FRIDA KAHLO

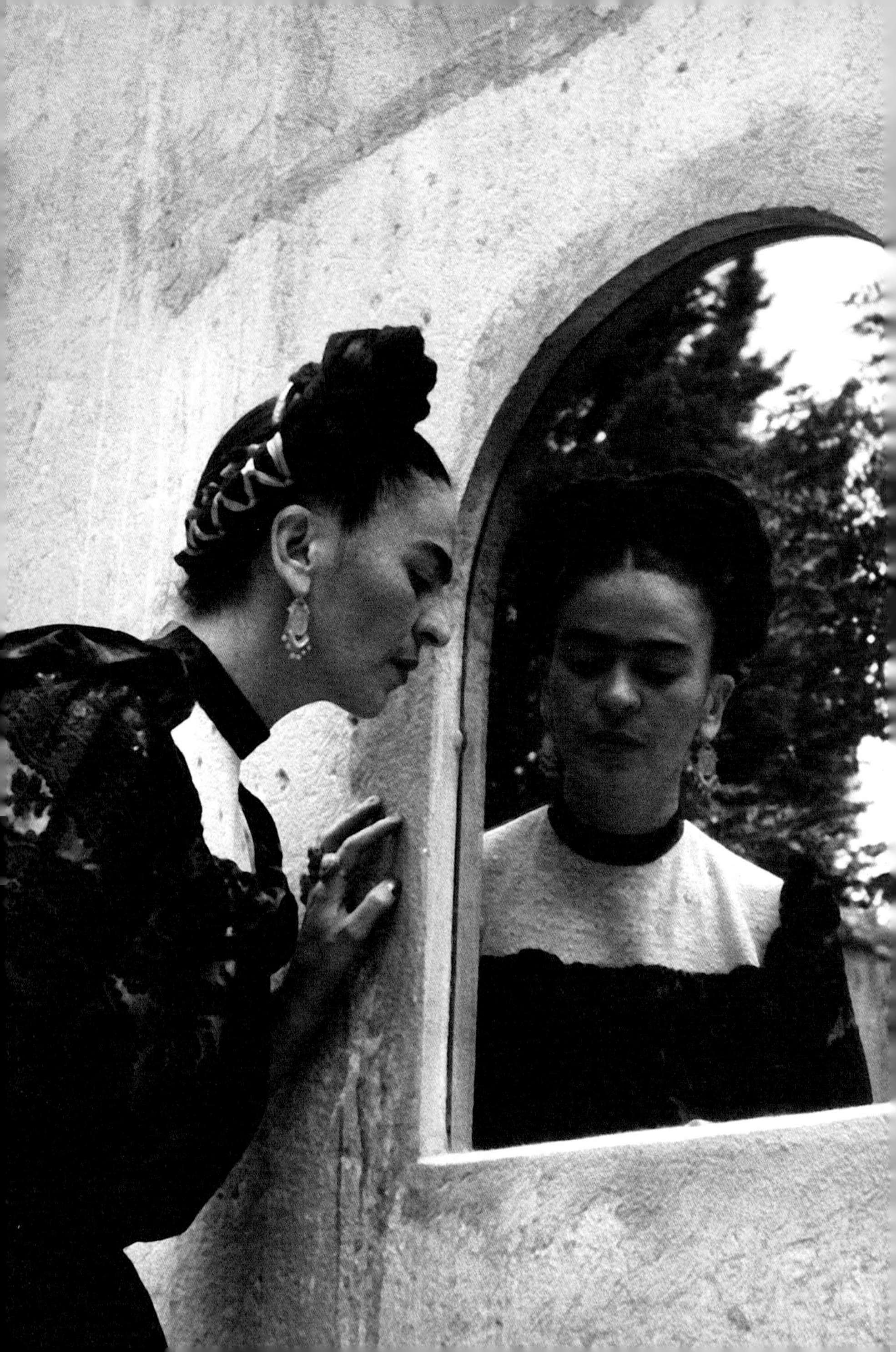

FRIDA KAHLO

BEATRIZ GARCÍA-VELASCO BERNAL

TATE

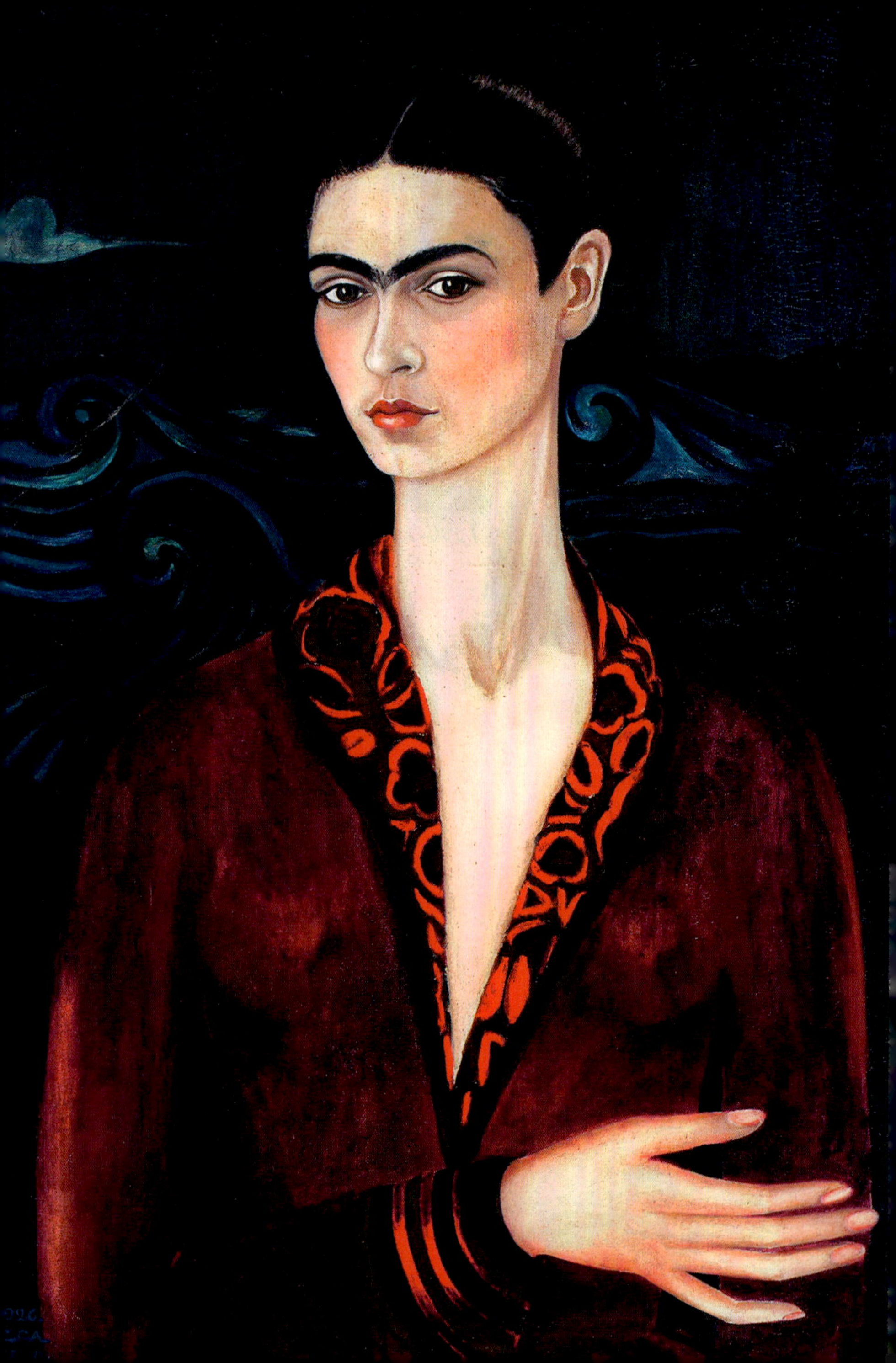

An enigmatic gaze, framed by a dark, heavy brow, cuts through the canvas, poised against a murky sea at dusk. The woman's features are elegant, stylised, her neck long and seductive as it descends into a plunging neckline. She is cloaked in velvet crimson, which reveals the soft contours of her breasts; her hand, an invitation, seems to gently caress her robe. The work is Frida Kahlo's first important self-portrait (opposite), painted in 1926, and dedicated to her boyfriend at the time, Alejandro Gómez Arias. Although Kahlo's pictorial language would radically shift in the following years, the work anticipates the artist's lifelong endeavour to reveal 'the frankest expression' of herself, or her multiple selves, to the world.[1]

Commanding, the single eyebrow divines the birth of the icon: Frida, the face that looks out from the canvas. Frida, the wife, the mestiza, the survivor. Frida, a pagan idol worshipped, reclaimed, consumed by a vast array of constituencies today. Fifty-five self-portraits make up a single image: a crown of flowers, an ancestral braid, a jade necklace, an open heart, a vine of thorns, roots, veins, ribbons, monkeys, parrots, cats, all entangled in Kahlo's infinite self. The self-portraits have been analysed through Kahlo's biography, her politics and even her psychology, regarded by some as a relatively minor product of bourgeois ideology or economic necessity and, at the other end of the spectrum, as products in and of themselves. Others are interested in Kahlo's construction of her personas, finding in the self-portraits an affirmation of othered identity that is uncompromisingly complex. Kahlo portrays herself as both the suffering body and the body irresistibly desired; the childless woman and the bearer of all living things; the devoted wife and the great master: 'the only person to give birth to herself', as her friend, the photographer Lola Álvarez Bravo, once said.[2]

Much of the power of the self-portraits lives in the force with which they crack open 'the spirit of a being', to quote another friend, the radical writer Nahui Olin: 'the power of expression, the vibrating restlessness, the constant rebellion of a spirit, of a brain in action endowed with thousands of microscopic fibres, sensitive to the contact of every living atom'.[3] They consist of multiple selves, 'millions of beings', Kahlo wrote, 'stones–bird creatures–star beings–microbe beings–fountain beings to ourselves'.[4] In the artist's cosmovision, she prevails as 'hate-love-mother-child-plant-earth-light-lightning-etc.,-world giver of worlds–universes and

Self-Portrait 1926
Oil paint on canvas
78.7 × 58.4

universal cells'.[5] 'The great concealer' defies us to penetrate the mask, even as she continually eludes us; to transcend the surface ('appearances can be deceiving', she cautions) (p.86); and to grapple with the multiplicity of a being who is broken but who also reigns supreme.[6] 'I, Frida Kahlo, paint myself, the image in the mirror.'[7]

TODAY STILL GOES ON

Kahlo had just turned nineteen when she executed *Self-Portrait* 1926 (p.4), shortly after suffering a serious accident that left her immobilised for almost a year. In September 1925, the bus in which she was riding with Gómez Arias collided into a trolley car (p.26). Kahlo was impaled by a metal handrail, which penetrated her pelvis and tore through her vagina. She fractured her spinal column, her collarbone and three vertebrae, as well as her right leg and foot, which was already affected by childhood polio. Kahlo never fully recovered from her injuries, undergoing around thirty-five surgeries and wearing orthopaedic corsets for the rest of her life. After the accident, Kahlo's mother had a special easel installed so Frida, confined to bed, could paint, with a mirror hanging from the canopy. From then on, the artist would continue to paint from the reflection of her image in the mirror; the series of extraordinary photographs by Álvarez Bravo of Kahlo looking at her reflection (frontispiece) acts as a portal into the workings of the artist's mirrored selves.

Despite the inexpressible agony, and periods of intolerable despair and boredom, Kahlo found strength in painting. She told Gómez Arias on the back of *Self-Portrait* 1926, 'Today still goes on'. Her early work reflects the influence of Renaissance painters such as Bronzino and Botticelli; from around 1926, Kahlo would depict her family and friends in a similar style, executing portraits of her sisters Adriana and Cristina, her neighbour Alicia Galant, her friend Ruth Quintanilla, as well as her 'cuates' from the Escuela Nacional Preparatoria, Gómez Arias, Miguel N. Lira and Jesús Ríos y Valle.[8]

Wanting to pursue a career in medicine, Kahlo had enrolled in the prestigious school at the age of fourteen, in 1922. She was one of only thirty-five girls in a cohort of two thousand students – her irreverence already visible from her student ID photograph, which shows Kahlo sporting a bob haircut popularised by Mexican flappers in the 1920s. Kahlo soon befriended class-mates from the intellectual bourgeoisie.[9] The group, known as Los Cachuchas from the unconventional caps they wore, were

Pancho Villa and Adelita
c.1927
Oil paint on canvas
65 × 45

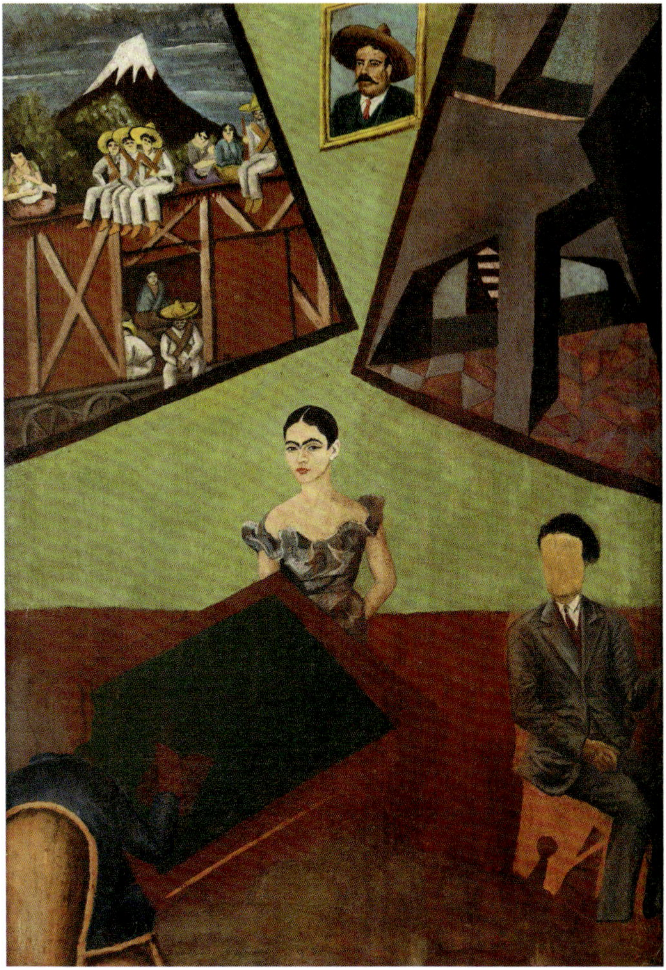

rebellious and carefree, and avid readers of poetry, literature and philosophy.

Kahlo depicted a Cachuchas-style gathering in the unfinished work *Pancho Villa and Adelita* c.1927 (above). Kahlo inscribes herself at the centre of the café scene, sitting next to an unidentified man. Above, two other compositions confront each other: to the left, 'soldaderas' (Mexican women fighters) and revolutionaries gather in a moving train, against the hills of rural Mexico. To the right, Kahlo renders an empty architectonic structure in a style reminiscent of cubism. The artist thus introduces a debate taking place in Mexican artistic and literary circles: whether to continue looking to Europe as the primary point of reference, or to adhere to the emerging nationalist celebration of their country's culture and pre-Hispanic heritage, fostered by the ideals of the Mexican Revolution (1910–20), known as 'mexicanidad'. Looking at this painting, Kahlo's allegiance becomes clear: the portrait of revolutionary leader Pancho Villa hangs at the centre of the composition.

Seven years before Kahlo painted *Pancho Villa and Adelita*, the revolutionaries had overthrown the conservative regime of Porfirio Díaz during the revolution. The new minister of education, José Vasconcelos, set out an ambitious educational and cultural programme across the country. He commissioned the artists David Alfaro Siqueiros, José Clemente Orozco and Diego Rivera to produce monumental frescoes in public spaces that embodied the social and political aspirations of the revolution and celebrated the spirit of 'mexicanidad'. It was one such commission that brought Kahlo and Rivera together for the first time: in 1922, Rivera began to work on the mural *The Creation* for the auditorium of the Preparatoria, where Kahlo would watch him paint. In 1928 their paths would cross again, most likely at one of the parties thrown by photographer and activist Tina Modotti, Kahlo's close friend and political comrade (both were members of the Young Communist League). That year, Kahlo and Modotti appeared in Rivera's mural *The Arsenal*, depicted as revolutionary fighters; by 1929, a forty-three-year-old Diego and a twenty-two-year-old Frida were married.

MEMORY

In the night, there sobbed a song ...
The Indians stretched, sinuously, through the narrow streets of the village. Wrapped in sarapes, swaying to the dance, after drinking mescal. The music came from a harp and a jaran, and the joy from dark-skinned smiling women.
In the background, behind the Zócalo, the river shimmered. And it moved on, like the minutes of my life.[10]

Kahlo's embrace of 'mexicanidad' has often been attributed to Rivera's influence. *Pancho Villa and Adelita*, however, demonstrates an interest in the Mexican vernacular at a time before Rivera, and 'Memory', the stridentist poem Kahlo published in 1922, shows an imaginary shaped by indigenous

Mexican culture, rituals and celebration, traditional costume, the sounds of popular music and corrido ballads, and the architectural make-up of the city, revealing a deep-rooted connection to the Mexican land. *Two Women (Salvadora and Herminia)* 1929 (below) reflects Kahlo's early engagement with Mexican folk traditions and the working class. The models are two Indigenous women who worked as maids at La Casa Azul, Kahlo's home in Coyoacán, on the outskirts of Mexico City. The artist depicts them in close proximity, solemn and self-assured, set against a backdrop of vibrant greenery.

Kahlo's fascination with pre-Hispanic culture shaped her work; her paintings are often set in the landscape of Mexico

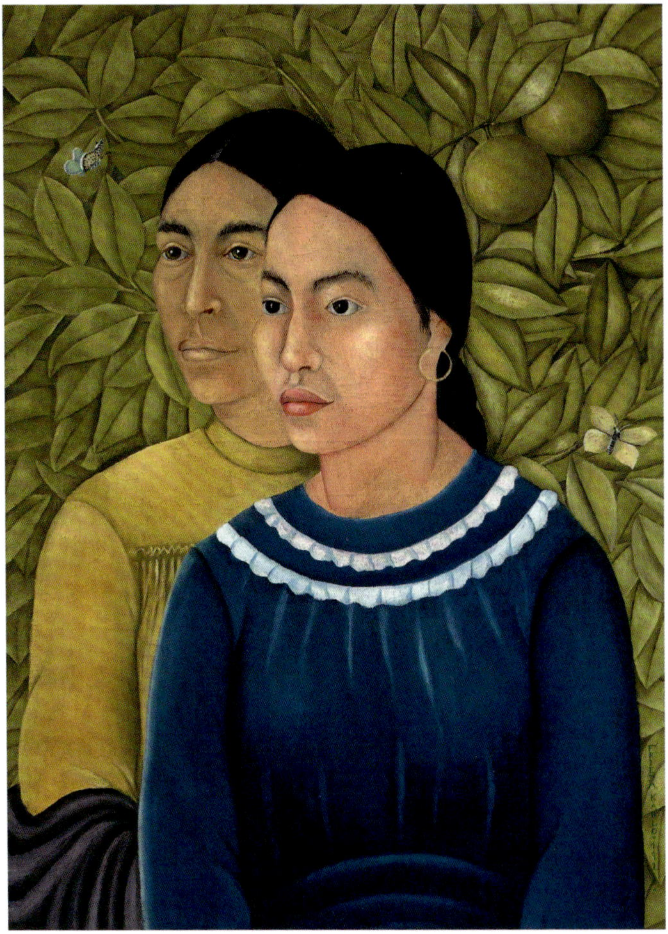

Two Women (Salvadora and Herminia) 1929
Oil paint on canvas
69.5 × 53.3

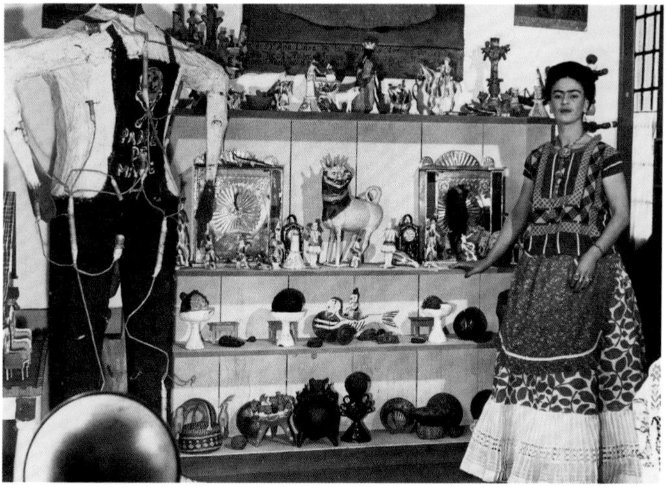

Kahlo in her living room at La Casa Azul c.1940

and reference vernacular forms and Aztec cosmologies. In *My Nurse and I* 1937 (pp.40–1), Kahlo portrays herself as a child being breastfed by her Indigenous maid, rendered as a pre-Hispanic fertility goddess; in *Four Inhabitants of Mexico* 1938 (pp.46–7), a young Frida appears in the Coyoacán Zócalo surrounded by archetypal motifs of Mexican culture: a Judas figure, a Nayarit sculpture, a skeleton characteristic of Day of the Dead celebrations, and a straw man – objects which she collected and lived with at La Casa Azul (above). Kahlo and Rivera would amass a rich collection of Olmec, Toltec and Aztec sculpture, which they would later house in the Anahuacalli Museum in Mexico City.

Kahlo's connection to ancestral Mexican culture was not just a political or artistic statement; it was an embodied reality and a spiritual lifeline. Nature, the entanglement of the human and the non-human and animist ontologies underpinned the artist's world-making and her conception of 'mexicanidad'. In that sense, Kahlo understood her position in the world as simultaneously rooted in her immediate regional context and in a universal order of things. References abound, but powerful examples include *Survivor* 1938 (p.44), *Portrait of Lucha Maria, A Girl from Tehuacán (Sun and Moon)* 1942 (p.62), *Self-Portrait with Small Monkey* 1945 (p.70) and *The Love Embrace of the Universe, the Earth (Mexico), Myself, Diego and Señor Xólotl* 1949 (p.24). Kahlo represented her identity as inextricably woven into the land and ecosystem of Mexico – a vision expressed in

My Grandparents, My Parents, and I 1936 (p.36), where Kahlo's biological roots are bound to the Mexican landscape by a red ribbon, which runs from her German, Spanish and Indigenous ancestors to the image of herself as a child.

Often mythologising her biography, Kahlo embodied her mestiza heritage by adopting traditional Mexican dress – a sartorial choice that, although popular among other Mexican female artists at the time, became inseparable from her persona. By 1934, the artist had appropriated the costumes of Tehuana women, very intentionally tapping into the myth of matriarchal utopia that was associated with the Zapotec people. The enagua, or long skirt, also helped conceal the physical effects of childhood polio on Kahlo's leg. The artist perpetuated this image of herself in her self-portraits but also through portraits that photographers and friends took of her. Among these, it is perhaps Nickolas Muray's photographs that most vividly capture Kahlo's intricate self-fashioning as the archetypal Mexican woman.

THE BORDER

From the winter of 1930 to the autumn of 1933, Kahlo and Rivera spent extended periods of time in the United States, following Rivera's mural commissions in San Francisco, New York and Detroit, and a solo exhibition at the Museum of Modern Art. Whereas Rivera was enthralled by the magnitude of US industry, envisioning technological progress at the service of the proletarian revolution, Kahlo remained openly critical of American capitalism. In letters to friends, she voiced her contempt for the elite circles she and Rivera were moving in, her dismay at the poverty they witnessed (fuelled by the Great Depression), and her growing sense of isolation, often referring to the US as 'Gringolandia'.[11] Although Kahlo made important connections and lasting friendships in the US, Rivera's acclaim led some people to regard her as simply the 'wife of the master mural painter [who] gleefully dabbles in works of art', as the headline of a 1933 Detroit news article read. 'Of course, he does pretty well for a little boy,' Kahlo told writer Florence Davies with her sardonic wit, 'but it is I who am the big artist.'[12]

Kahlo produced major works during her time in the US. Two of them, *Self-Portrait on the Border Line Between Mexico and the United States* 1932 (p.12) and *My Dress Hangs There* 1933 (pp.28–9), offer a harsh commentary on American capitalism. In *Self-Portrait on the Border Line*, Kahlo constructs a visual landscape

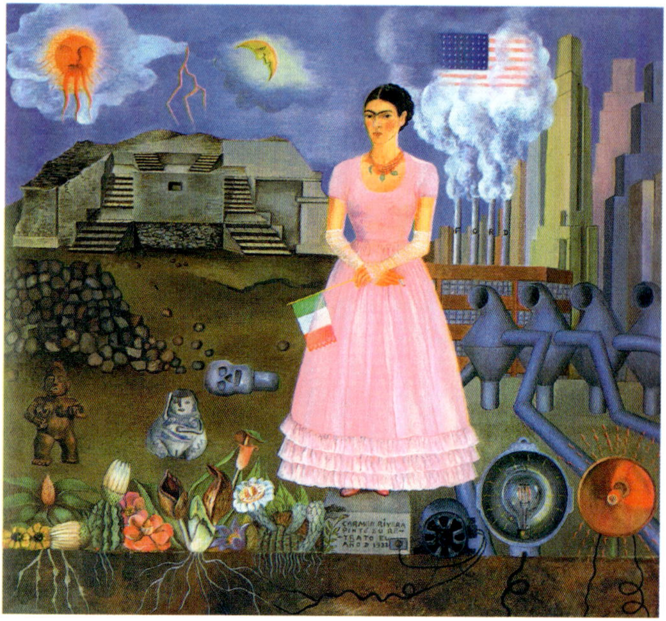

Self-Portrait on the Border Line Between Mexico and the United States 1932
Oil paint on metal
31.8 × 34.9

of oppositions between Mexico as the ancestral land and the US as industrial machine. Wearing a pink gown and holding a Mexican flag, Kahlo positions herself as a literal border, a symbolic gesture of non-belonging that feels all the more timely today. At her feet, tropical flowers spring from clay-brown earth, while technological devices plug into American soil. Above her, the dual cosmologies of the sun and the moon preside over the sky, whose clouds contrast with the billowing smoke that lifts aloft the American flag. An Aztec temple sits alongside the skyline of a barren US, where factories and skyscrapers erode nature and serve as new objects of devotion and national pride.

Kahlo's time in the United States was also marked by a life-threatening miscarriage, which caused her severe haemorrhaging. In July 1932, after two and a half months in Detroit, she was hospitalised. During her recovery, the artist produced her first work on metal, *Henry Ford Hospital* 1932 (opposite), borrowing from the tradition of Mexican devotional paintings known as 'ex-votos' or 'retablos'. This popular art form, which Kahlo avidly collected and embraced as one of her signature formats, typically depicts recovery from illness, potential accidents or other hardships and is created as an offering of gratitude for miraculous intervention. The artist, fascinated by medical illustrations since childhood, incorporated anatomical studies of the female reproductive system that Rivera sourced for her during her stay in hospital. The work is remarkably candid in its depiction of the suffering female body: Kahlo lies naked on a hospital bed soaked in a crimson pool of blood, looking unusually small, her knees drawn up as she cradles her belly. A tear slashes her cheek; from her hand a network of veins branches out and connects to six symbolic images: a female reproductive system, an unborn foetus, a snail, Kahlo's broken pelvic bone, an orchid and a sterilising instrument. In the distance, Kahlo depicts Detroit's skyline as a marker of time and place.

Kahlo thus reclaims a subject long stigmatised – women's inability to conceive – and renders it not in the style of a romanticised nativity, but rather through imagery evocative of Christ's martyrdom.[13] During the same period, Kahlo executed another ex-voto and one of her most hauntingly powerful works, *My Birth* 1932 (pp.32–3), coinciding with the death of her mother, just months after Kahlo's miscarriage. She depicts a woman lying on a bed, knees raised, her face covered by a white sheet. Her vagina is torn open, the exposed labia rendered with anatomical precision, from which the head of a young Kahlo – recognisable by her single eyebrow – emerges. A painting of

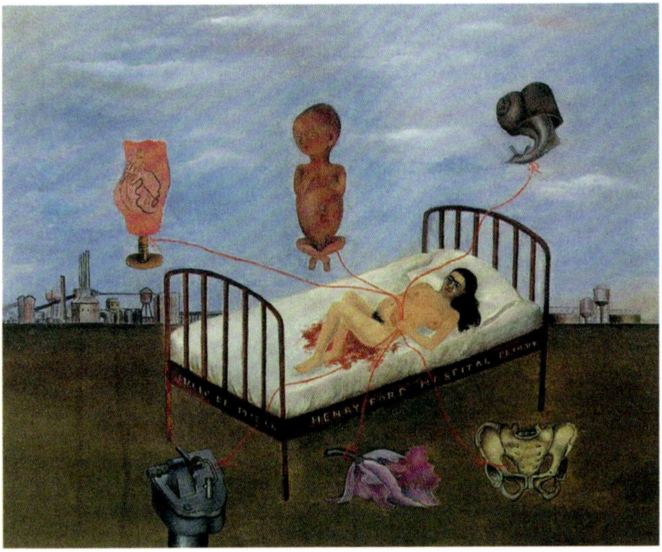

Henry Ford Hospital 1932
Oil paint on metal
30.5 × 38

the Virgin of Sorrows hangs above; below, a white strip mirrors the section where devotees write their thanks to the saints in ex-votos, which Kahlo leaves blank. The grotesque quality of Kahlo's work resides not so much in its directness or in its unfiltered portrayal of childbirth, but in the presence of the shrouded figure and its implications of death. Kahlo identified the figure as her mother, but also, crucially, as herself. Depicting yet another taboo scene of female sexuality, Kahlo introduces a play of doubles, a strategy that she would continue to employ in her work: the mother and child, life and death, fertility and barrenness.[14] Yet Kahlo complicates these binaries by depicting herself in the act of self-birth, thus executing her first double self-portrait, preceding the monumental *The Two Fridas* 1939 (pp.54–5).

DIVERSITY IN UNITY

The play of doubles and oppositions in Kahlo's work is intimately linked to her exploration of identity and her mirrored selves, exemplified by *The Two Fridas*, in which the Tehuana and the normative, bourgeois Frida sit hand in hand. In *Tree of Hope* 1946 (p.78), Kahlo portrays her two personas under the opposing symbols of the sun and the moon: the suffering body, split open like the cracks in the land, and its counterpart, the unyielding bearer of life.

Throughout her work, Kahlo assumed different roles and challenged traditional expectations of womanhood. Examples include the suckling child in *My Nurse and I* (pp.40–1), the devoted Mexican wife in *Frieda and Diego Rivera* 1931 (p.27),[15] the failed mother in *Henry Ford Hospital* (p.13), the adulterer in *Self-Portrait Dedicated to Leon Trotsky* 1937 (p.38), the chaste nun in *Diego on My Mind (Self-Portrait as Tehuana)* 1943 (p.16) and the mother-goddess in *The Love Embrace of the Universe* (p.24).[16]

Subverting conservative gender roles in Mexican society at the time, *Self-Portrait with Cropped Hair* 1940 (opposite) depicts an androgynous Kahlo, dressed in men's clothing. Her locks of hair are strewn across the composition; we know she is the perpetrator because she holds a pair of scissors. Above, Kahlo inscribes the score of a corrido with the lyrics: 'If I ever loved you, it was because of your hair. Now that you're bald, I don't love you anymore.' The work is often read in relation to Kahlo and Rivera's divorce the previous year, when Kahlo cut her hair to scorn her husband, who was having an affair with her sister Cristina. But it also demonstrates the artist's experimentation

Self-Portrait with Cropped Hair 1940
Oil paint on canvas
40 × 28

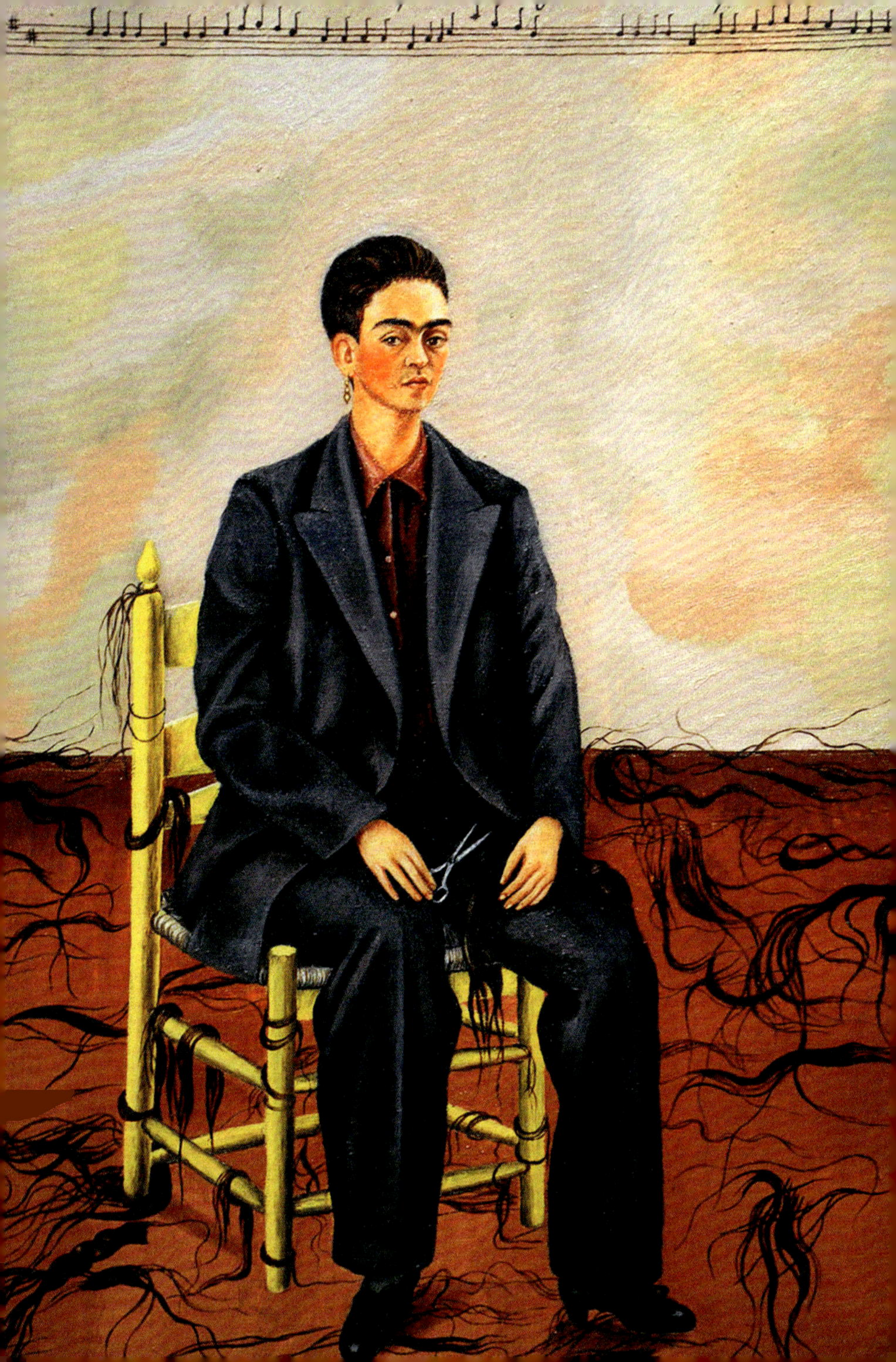

Diego on My Mind (Self-Portrait as Tehuana) 1943
Oil paint on masonite
76 × 61

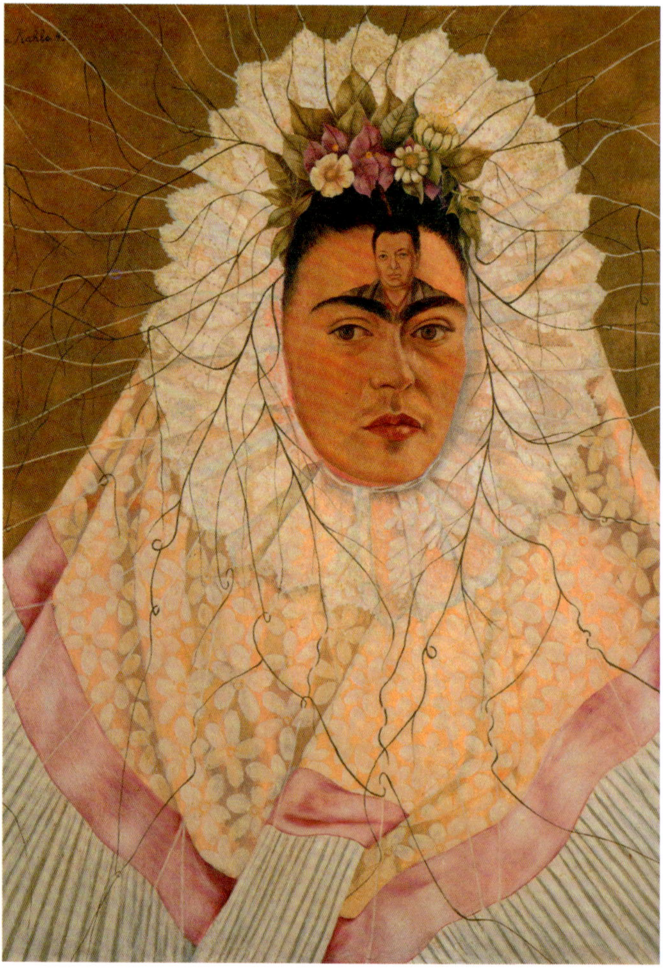

with gender hybridity and cross dressing, and symbolises her economic and emotional emancipation from Rivera.[17] After moving out of their shared house in San Ángel that year, and taking an apartment in the city, Kahlo wrote to him: 'I'll pay my way with painting and then even if I have to swallow shit, I'll do whatever I fancy whenever I fancy.'[18]

Although Kahlo did not share her husband's economic independence, she did experience a degree of sexual freedom, engaging in numerous affairs with both men and women – among them, Soviet politician Leon Trotsky, artist Isamu Noguchi and singer Chavela Vargas. *Two Nudes in a Forest* 1939 (pp.48–9) is one of Kahlo's most erotically charged works, depicting a white woman and a brown woman caressing each other naked in a fertile Eden set on Mexican soil. This dual figure previously appeared in *What the Water Gave Me* 1938 (p.19), a work the artist described as an expression of her daydreams and masturbatory fantasies.[19] Kahlo surrounded herself with empowered women and radical female artists, including Lucienne Bloch, Tina Modotti, Lola Álvarez Bravo, Dolores del Río, Rosa Rolanda and María Felix, nurturing long-lasting friendships that had a profound influence on her: some of their names can still be read painted on the walls of her bedroom at La Casa Azul.

Despite their tumultuous marriage – marked by a divorce, remarriage, several separations and countless affairs – Kahlo's emotional, artistic and intellectual relationship with Rivera remained a vital pillar of her life until her death. They admired and championed each other's work, stimulating a shared passion for the Mexican vernacular, pre-Hispanic culture, socialism, music and parties. The extent of Kahlo's all-consuming love for Rivera is reflected in several paintings; in two of these, *Diego on My Mind (Self-Portrait as Tehuana)* (opposite) and *Diego and I* 1949 (p.80), the artist depicts Rivera on her forehead as a third eye, referencing Hindu, Buddhist and Tao spiritualism. The artist regarded her relationship with Rivera as ontological, vitally linked to her own existence, rooted to the land and all earthly beings, a force that transcended the physical self and defied the rot of time. 'My blood is the miracle that travels in the veins of the air from my heart to yours', she wrote in her diary.[20] Another page reads:

> Diego beginning
> Diego constructor
> Diego my baby
> Diego my boyfriend
> Diego painter
> Diego my lover
> Diego 'my husband'
> Diego my friend
> Diego my mother
> Diego = me =
> Diego Universe
> Diversity in unity.[21]

WHAT THE WATER GAVE ME

In January 1937, Kahlo greeted Leon Trotsky and his wife Natalia Sedova at the pier in Tampico. They moved into La Casa Azul, where they stayed until Trotsky's assassination in 1940. During that time, Kahlo and Trotsky had a brief but passionate affair; he wrote numerous letters to her, and she dedicated a self-portrait to him (p.38), where she depicts herself standing between open curtains, her hair adorned in flowers and ribbons, and holding a bouquet and a letter, which reads: 'To Leon Trotsky, with all my love'. Eager to meet the Soviet revolutionary, French surrealist André Breton and his wife, the artist Jacqueline Lamba, arrived soon after, encountering Kahlo's work for the first time. Breton admired her work and hailed her as a surrealist; an invitation from Julien Levy, a US gallerist and advocate of surrealism, for a solo show in his New York gallery soon followed. 'There is no art more exclusively feminine,' commented Breton on the essay to accompany the exhibition, 'in the sense that, in order to be as seductive as possible, it is only too willing to play alternatively at being absolutely pure and absolutely pernicious. The art of Frida Kahlo is a ribbon around a bomb.'[22] More interesting than Breton's essentialist view of femininity is his recognition of the sheer force of Kahlo's paintings – modest in scale, yet powerfully confrontational.

In 1939, Breton organised the *Mexique* exhibition at the Galerie Renou & Colle in Paris, which included eighteen works by Kahlo as well as photographs by Manuel Álvarez Bravo and pre-Hispanic objects and popular artefacts from Mexico. It was there that the Jeu de Paume acquired *The Frame* 1938 (p.51). In Paris, Kahlo met members of the European surrealist circle, including Marcel Duchamp, Pablo Picasso, Joan Miró, Paul Éluard, Max Ernst and Wassily Kandinsky. However, and with the exception of Duchamp, Kahlo did not take to the group; she found 'the surrealist turds', as she referred to them in her private letters, pretentious and out of touch with the escalating political tensions in Europe.[23] Back in Mexico City, however, Kahlo was invited to show her work at the 1940 International Exhibition of Surrealism, organised by artists César Moro and Wolfgang Paalen at the Inés Amor gallery, and she produced *The Two Fridas* for the event.

Despite her association with transnational surrealist circles, Kahlo never adhered to the movement, seeing her work not as an expression of the irrational, but as a reflection

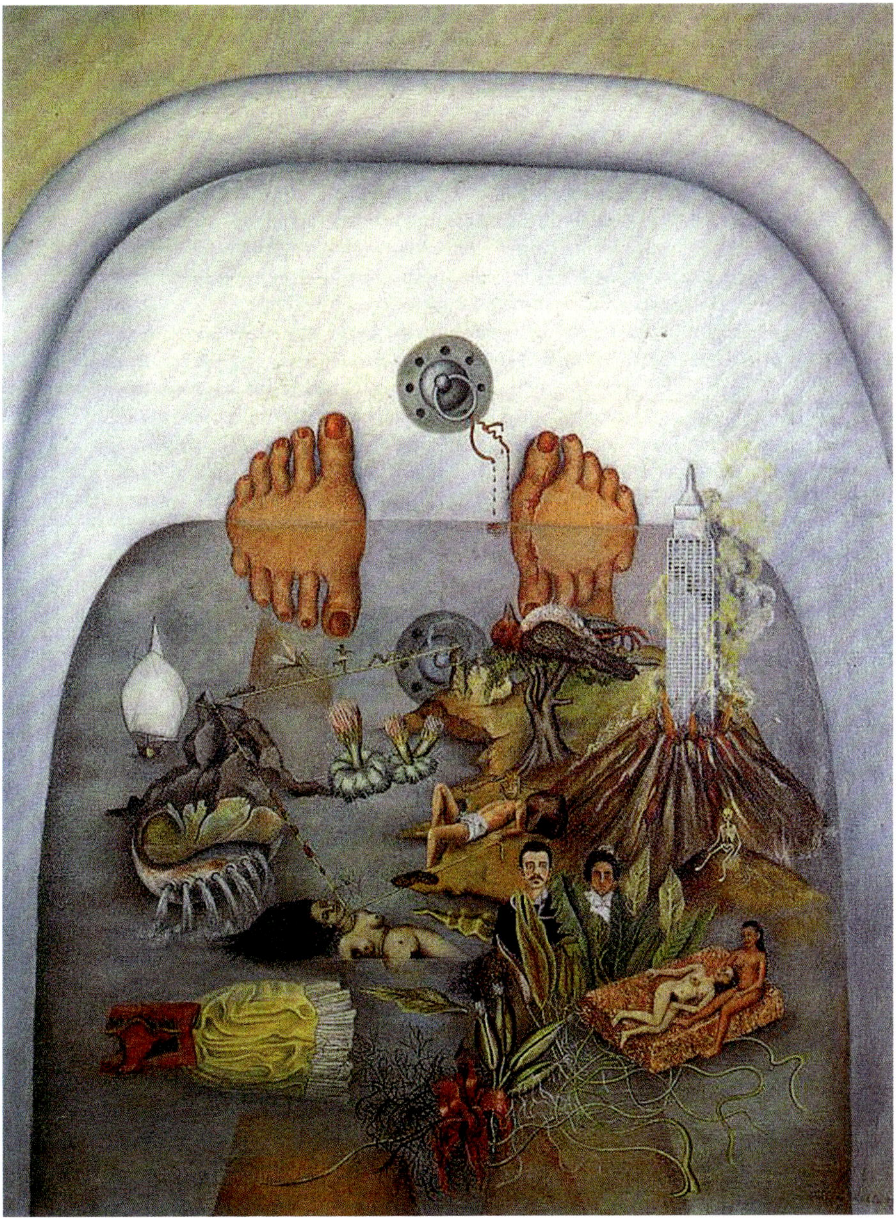

What the Water Gave Me 1938
Oil paint on canvas
91 × 70.5

of her lived experience. Yet in *What the Water Gave Me* (p.19), Kahlo projects her inner self, her dreams, desires and obsessions, showing clear parallels with Freudian theories of the unconscious and the pleasure principle. The painting depicts Kahlo's legs submerged in a bathtub, viewed from the perspective of the artist looking down towards her feet while bathing. Mirroring the semi-conscious state of daydreaming, Kahlo inverts the verticality of the gaze to present a full frontal of her toes emerging from a dizzying landscape. The water invokes a constellation of images: her Tehuana dress, her parents as pictured in their wedding photograph, the female lovers that would appear in *Two Nudes in a Forest*, a volcano erupting around the Empire State Building, a lone naked woman, an anthropomorphous seashell in the style of Hieronymus Bosch and an assortment of animal and plant life, connected through roots and vines.

TREE OF HOPE

After Trotsky's assassination in 1940, Kahlo was arrested and interrogated. Her health had deteriorated and Rivera, who had fled Mexico fearing prosecution by the authorities, asked her to join him in San Francisco, where she was duly hospitalised for a month. They remarried that year and eventually moved back in together at La Casa Azul. Kahlo would spend the remaining years of her life intermittently bedridden, bound to a succession of orthopaedic corsets, surgeries and medical treatments which did not, however, prevent her from painting and continuing to gain recognition in Mexico. In 1943, Kahlo was offered a teaching position at the liberal arts school La Esmeralda in Mexico City. As her health worsened, she held her classes at home, teaching her students – later known as Los Fridos – to paint from their immediate surroundings: her garden, the objects she had collected and elements of popular Mexican culture, including retablo paintings and pulquería taverns, as well as pre-Hispanic art, anatomy and the Mexican and European avant-garde. That same year, Kahlo organised a mural commission at the pulquería La Rosita for her students, with a lively opening attended by members of the Mexican intelligentsia, featuring mariachis, dancing and corridos.

The Broken Column 1944
Oil paint on masonite
39.8 × 30.5

'Tree of hope, stand firm' reads the banner that Kahlo holds in *Tree of Hope* (p.78). 'Don't let your eyes cry when I leave, sweet darling, as I say goodbye', continues the popular

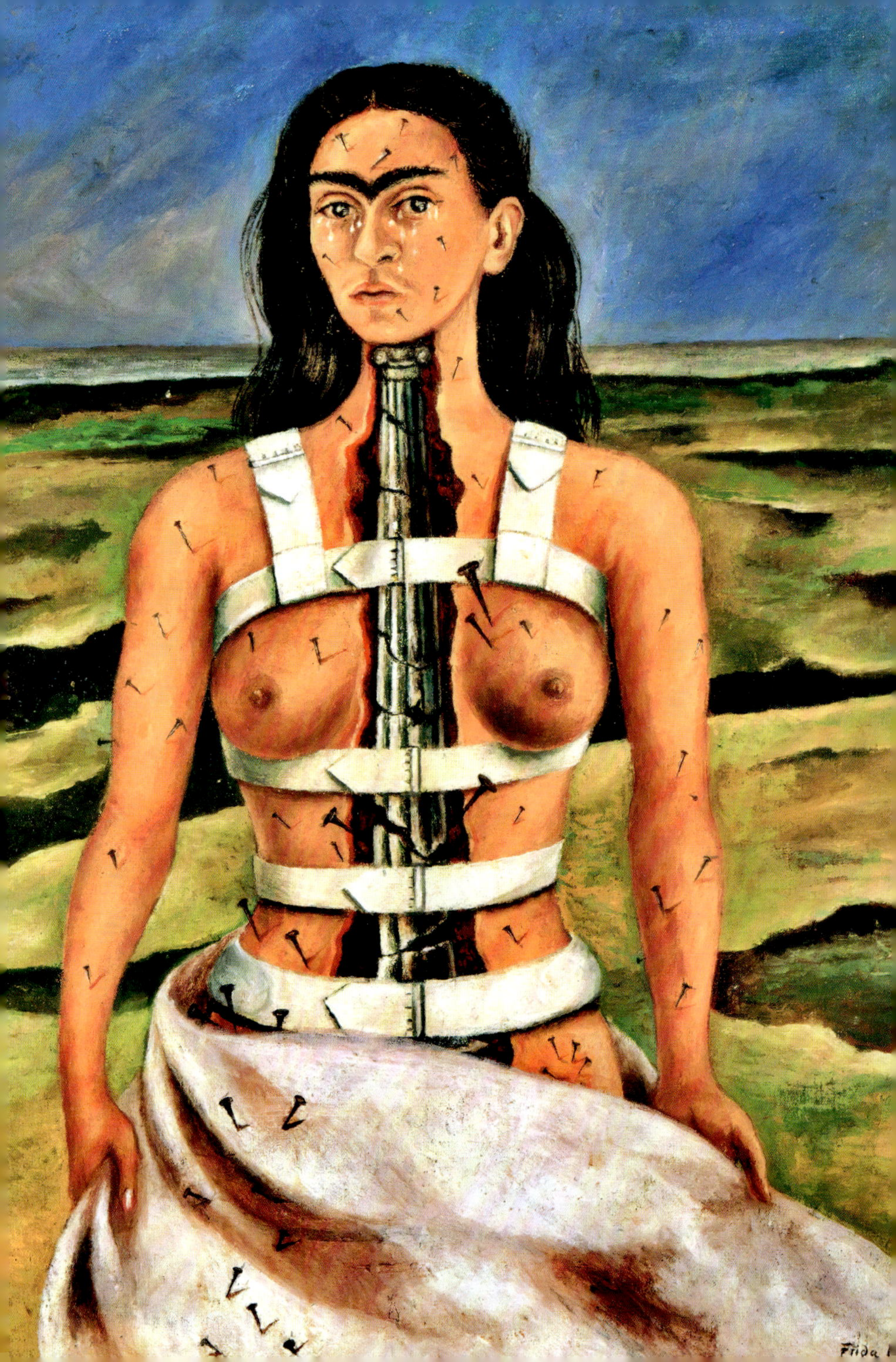
Frida

Mexican ballad, which Kahlo enjoyed singing. In the 1940s, she produced some of her most poignant works depicting her disability and suffering. Created during a period when she had to be force-fed, *Without Hope* 1945 (pp.74–5) depicts the artist bedridden in the Mexican landscape, a funnel-cum-visceral substance filled with vegetables, dead animals and formless organic matter excreting from her mouth. In *The Broken Column* 1944 (p.21), Kahlo cracks herself open. She portrays herself naked from the waist up, wearing an orthopaedic corset, her torso sutured open to reveal an Ionic column in place of her spine, fractured and on the verge of collapse. Echoing the iconography of Christ's crucifixion, her flesh is pierced by nails, while her eyes look out in a profound lament, tears streaming down her face. Kahlo noted in her diary, 'To hope with anguish retained, the broken column, and the immense look, without walking, in the vast path ... moving my life created of steel.'[24]

Kahlo's lifelong struggle with chronic illness and life-threatening surgeries partly explains her fascination with death. In 1943 she portrayed herself *Thinking About Death* (p.66); earlier she had painted a postmortem portrait of *The Deceased Dimas Rosas (at Three Years of Age)* 1937 (p.37) in the style of folk Mexican tributes; then there was *Girl with Death Mask* in 1938 (p.45). Death was also a significant aspect of Mexican popular consciousness and tradition, famously expressed in the Day of the Dead celebrations, and a recurring theme among Kahlo's contemporaries. It was a central motif in the work of José Guadalupe Posada, an earlier-generation satirical cartoonist whose work was later embraced by revolutionary artists and whom Kahlo greatly admired. His sensationalist, crude imagery and sarcastic language is echoed more forcefully in Kahlo's *A Few Small Nips* 1935 (pp.34–5). The work depicts a woman lying naked on a bed, her body slashed with multiple stab wounds, while a man stands over her holding a knife. The bed and the floor are covered in blood, which spills in spatters of red paint onto the frame. Kahlo based the work on a news account of gender violence; in court, the assassin had declared, 'But I just gave her a couple of little nips!' Kahlo used a similar trompe-l'oeil effect in *The Suicide of Dorothy Hale* 1938–9 (p.53), where the blood that spills from Hale's dead body seeps in vein-like form onto the frame.

In other works, blood and veins become roots that travel through Kahlo's body from the earth to the cosmos. In her erotically charged 'alive still lifes', as she called them, tears, semen and breast milk spurt from nature and microscopic organisms to produce nourishment; vines and leaves act as the backdrop of most of the artist's self-portraits and as the backbone of Kahlo's conception of being.[25] The artist regarded death as a return to the earth – part of the infinite interconnectedness of all living things, where decomposition nourishes the land. This duality draws from Aztec mythology, epitomised by the mother goddess Coatlicue, who embodies death and rebirth, as well as Buddhist, Hindu and Tao spiritualism, which Kahlo avidly studied in the later years of her life.[26] She liked to coexist among human and non-human beings, sharing her house and garden with monkeys, dogs, parrots and a fawn. Their significance to her is evident in how often Kahlo portrayed them in her work, always in close proximity or entangled with her (pp.42–3, 52, 58, 61, 63–4, 70). She kept Xoloitzcuintli dogs (guides to the underworld, according to pre-Hispanic belief), and named one of them Señor Xólotl after the dog-headed Aztec deity.

In *Roots* 1943 (pp.68–9) Kahlo's bed becomes the arid Mexican soil, and her broken truncal column a thick vine, its leaves entangled with her veins as they take root in the earth. After a spinal fusion surgery in 1946, which marked the beginning of her physical decline, Kahlo portrayed herself in *The Wounded Deer* 1946 (pp.76–7) as an anthropomorphous creature, half human, half deer. In the place of her usual crown of flowers, her human head bears a pair of large antlers, while her animal torso is pierced by arrows, echoing the iconography of Saint Sebastian. At the lower left corner of the canvas, Kahlo inscribed the word 'Carma [sic]', referring to the cycle of rebirth in Hindu spiritualism.

But perhaps the most monumental expression of Kahlo's cosmovision is *The Love Embrace of the Universe* (p.24). Kahlo is portrayed cradling a naked, infant-like Rivera, while she herself is held by an earth goddess, whose mossy-green body bears cacti, trees and flora associated with the Mexican landscape, as well as a network of veiny roots. They are all embraced in the mighty arms of a cosmic force, an incarnation of the dual cosmologies of the sun and the moon; Kahlo's dog Señor Xólotl rests peacefully on one of her arms. Kahlo thus presents

The Love Embrace of the Universe, the Earth (Mexico), Myself, Diego and Señor Xólotl
1949
Oil paint on canvas
70 × 60.5

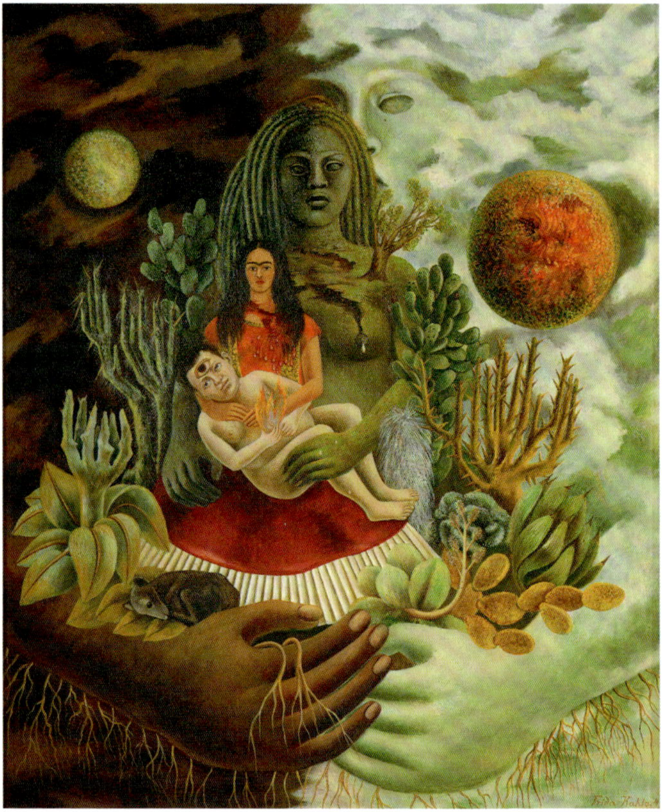

a matriarchal creation myth where she is also the mother, 'the grandmother, the Ancient Concealer', as she wrote, 'the necessary and eternal matter, the mother of men, and all the gods invented by them in their delirium ... THE WOMAN, and among all of them – I MYSELF'.[27]

In 1953, Kahlo's health had badly deteriorated, leading to the amputation of her leg due to gangrene. 'Feet, what do I want them for, if I have wings to fly?' she wrote in her diary (p.87).[28] In April that year, her friend Lola Álvarez Bravo organised Kahlo's first monographic show in Mexico. Kahlo arrived in an ambulance, then lay in the gallery in her four-poster bed. The show – a farewell of sorts – was attended by her friends, artists, writers, but also crowds of people from outside the visual arts world. Kahlo died the following year. Eight days before her death, she had written the words 'Viva La Vida' on a slice of watermelon depicted in what would be her last 'alive still life' (pp.88–9). That year she also painted *Marxism Will Give Health to the Sick* (p.83), a work that expresses Kahlo's vision of socialism as a force of healing and liberation. In her 'profound desire to help transform the society in which [she] lived', Kahlo dreamed of 'a great fiesta in which each and every being took part'; she wrote, 'from men to stones, suns and shadows: all cooperating with their own beauty and creative power'.[29] More than half a century later, Kahlo's commitment to social change and animist world-making continues to feel radical today.

'Can verbs be invented?' Kahlo asked in a letter to her friend the poet Carlos Pellicer. 'I want to say one to you: I *sky* you, so my wings stretch out enormously to love you without measure.'[30] At her funeral, Pellicer replied with a sonnet dedicated to the artist:

> If in your womb camped the prodigious
> rose of colours, if your breasts
> nourish the earth with dusky
> provisions of luminous density;
> if from your maternal vastness
> the nocturnal rose of holy nights
> drew that-image of yourself with serene
> disasters crossing your populous face;
> if your children were born with ages
> that no one can supply with hours
> because they speak the solitude of eternities,
> you will always remain upon the living earth,
> you will always be a mutiny full of dawns,
> the heroic flower of successive dawns.[31]

THE LAST INVOCATION

In Kahlo's last self-portrait, *Self-Portrait with the Portrait of Doctor Farill* 1951 (pp.84–5), she sits in a wheelchair, her heart on her palette. That poignant metaphor is a testament to how Kahlo regarded her art as a vital part of her existence, the blood that pumped through her veins. In a letter to Gómez Arias, the artist dreamed of being a 'tiny little thing that you could just carry around in your pocket forever and ever'.[32] Although much has been written about the artist's work, this publication is a modest invitation for readers to delve into Kahlo's world, to continue engaging with her work in new ways, and to carry with them a small piece of the monument that is Frida Kahlo.

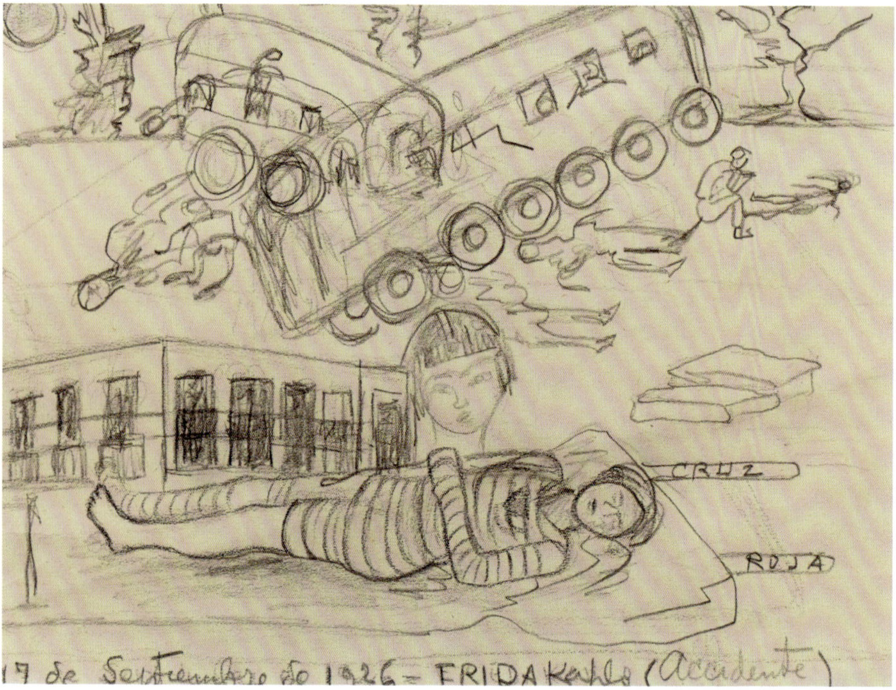

The Accident 1926
Graphite on paper
18.5 × 25.8

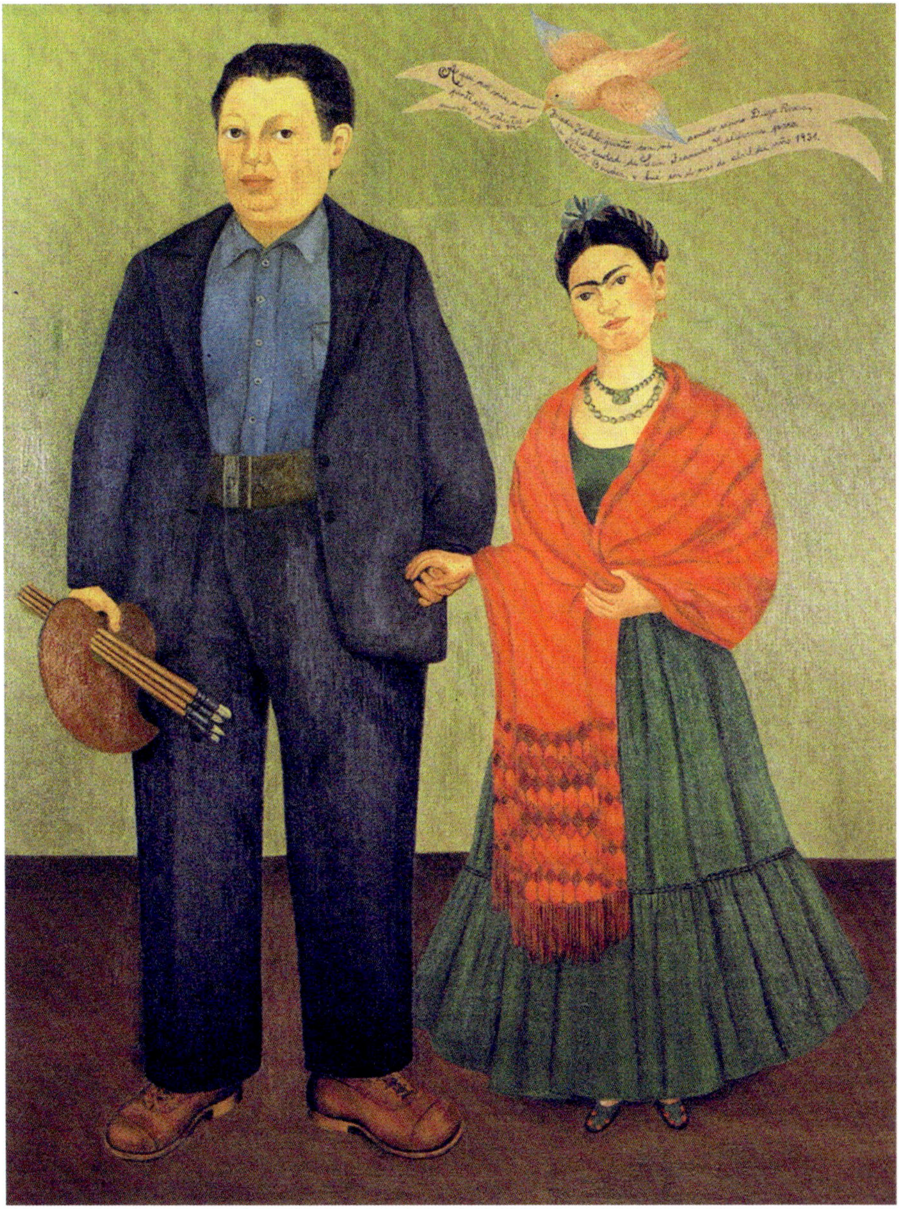

Frieda and Diego Rivera 1931
Oil paint on canvas
100 × 78.7

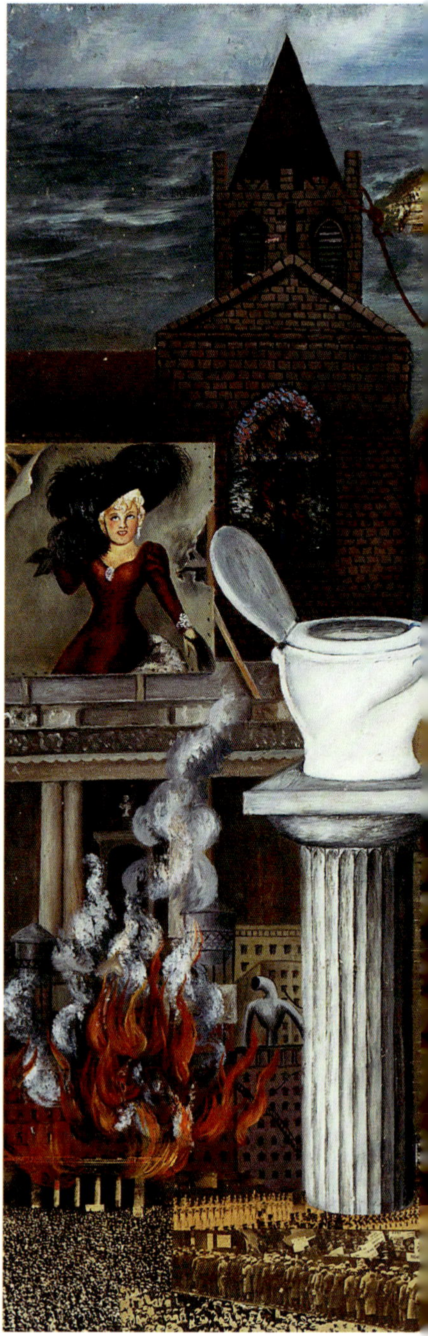

My Dress Hangs There 1933
Oil paint and collage on masonite
46 × 50

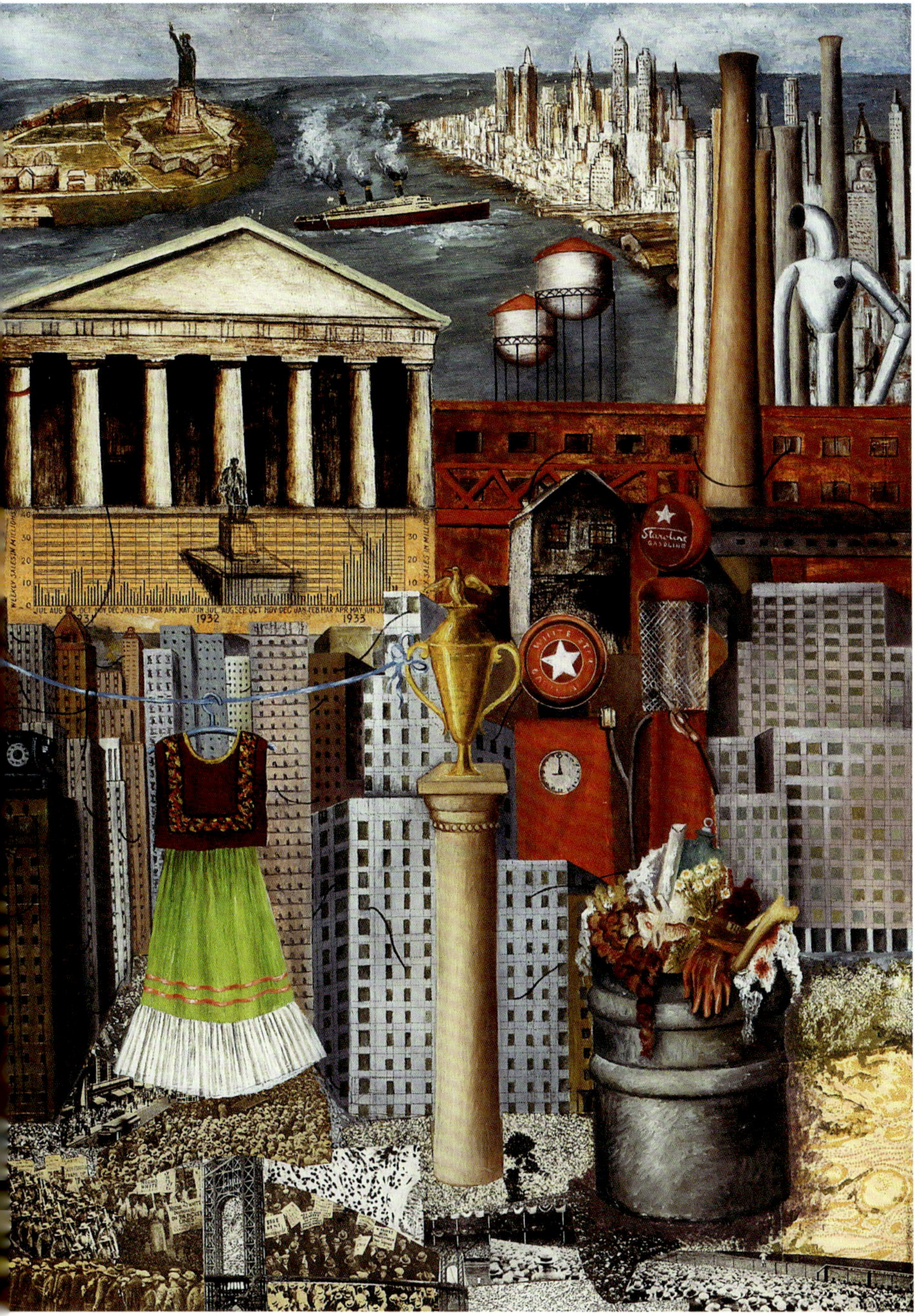
1932
1933

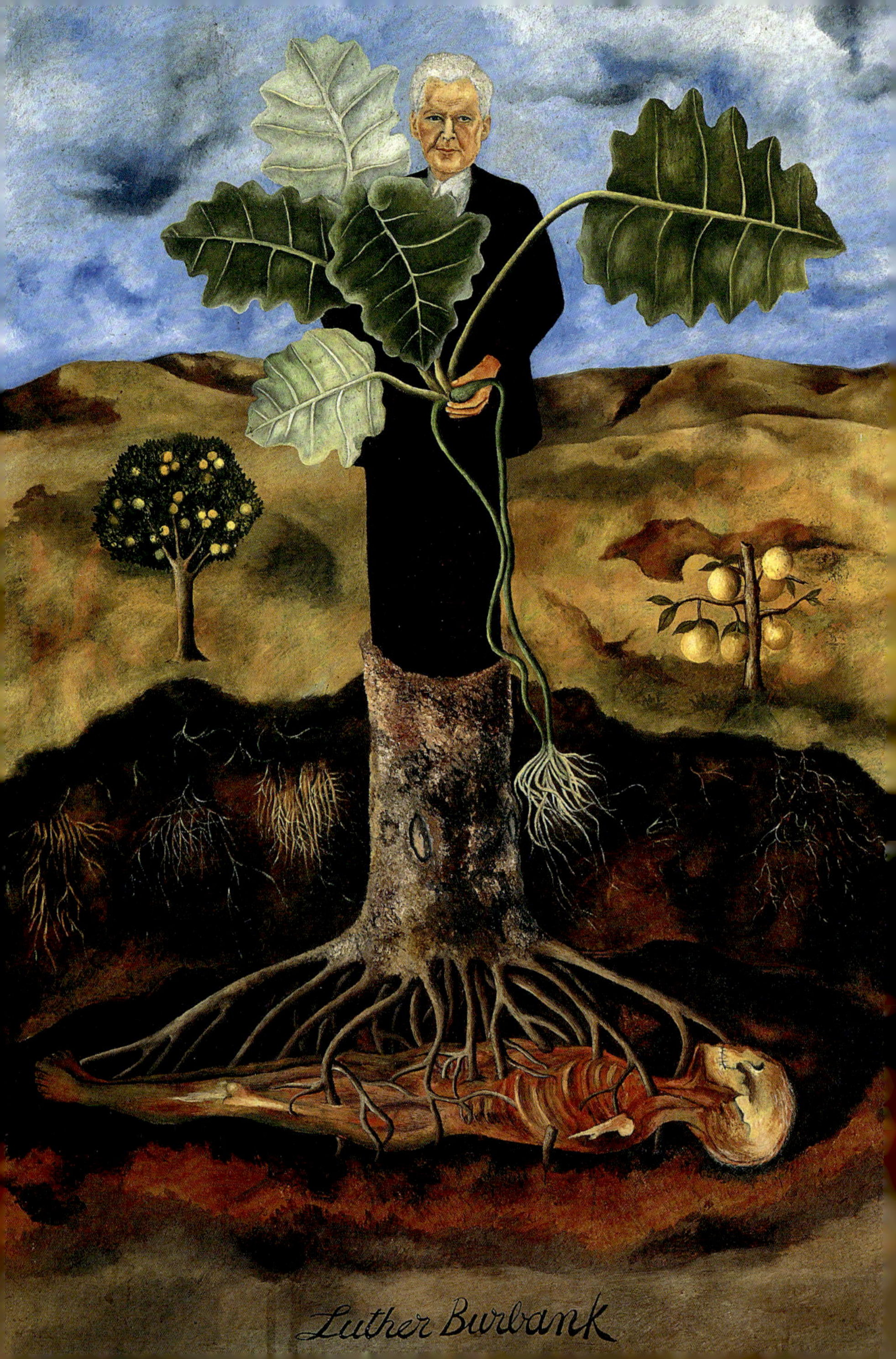
Luther Burbank

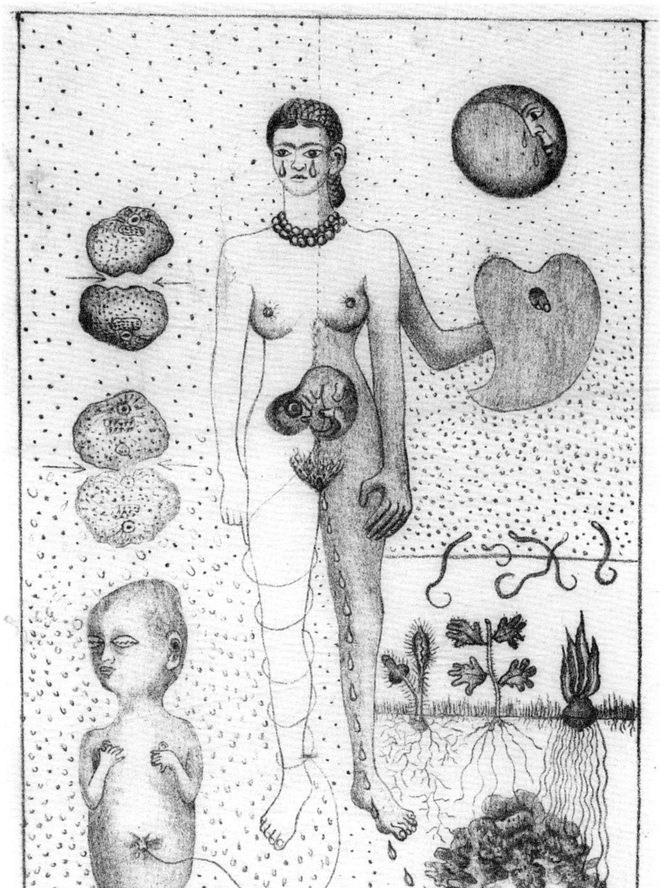

Portrait of Luther Burbank 1931
Oil paint on masonite
87 × 62

El Aborto (Frida and the Miscarriage) 1932
Lithograph on paper
22.2 × 14.2

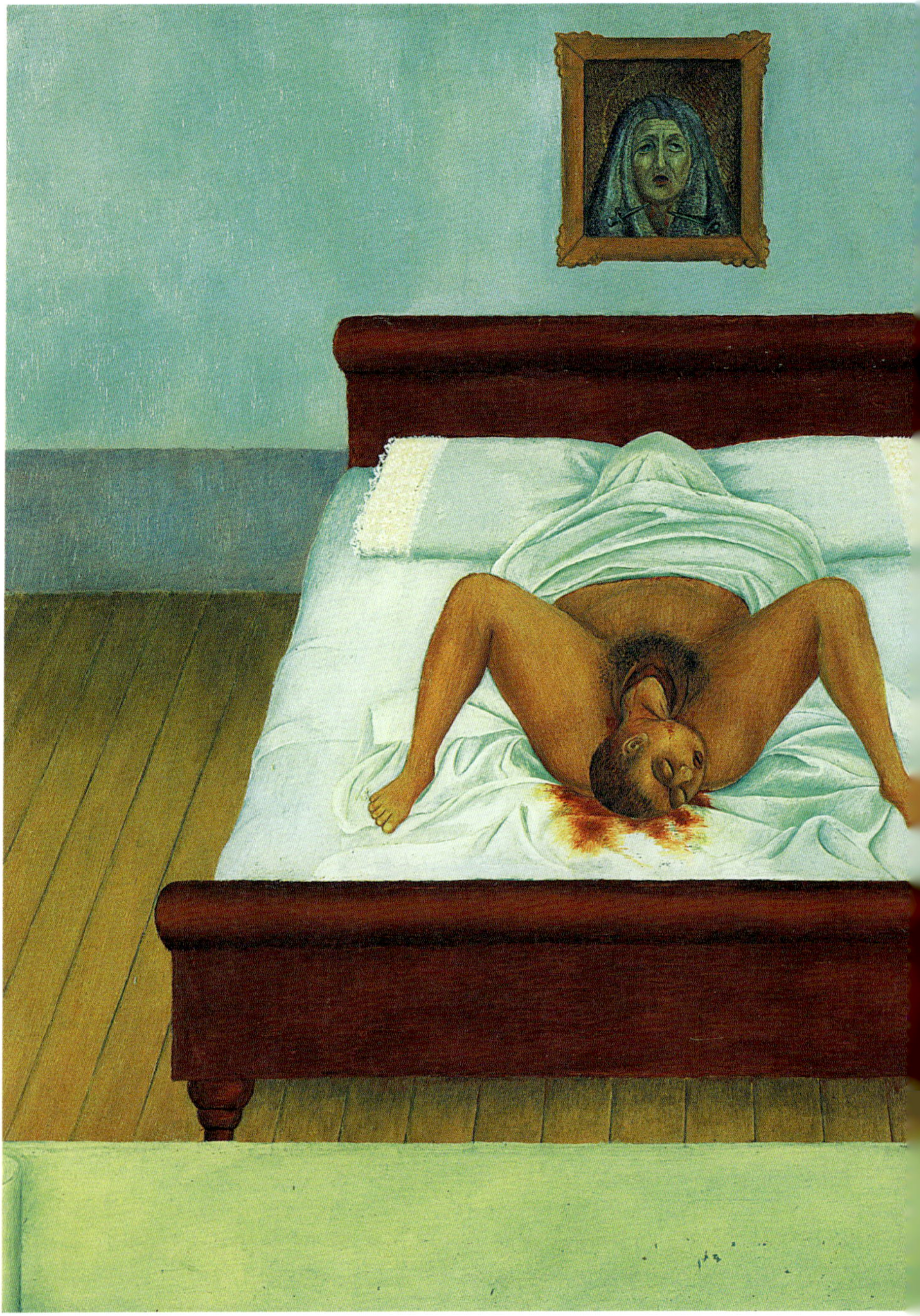

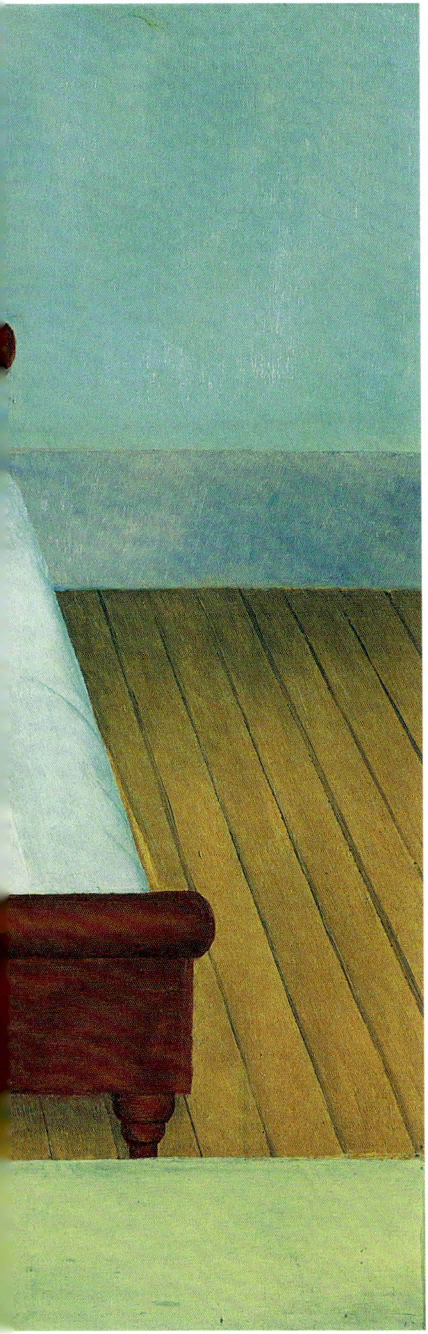

My Birth 1932
Oil paint on copper
30.5 × 85

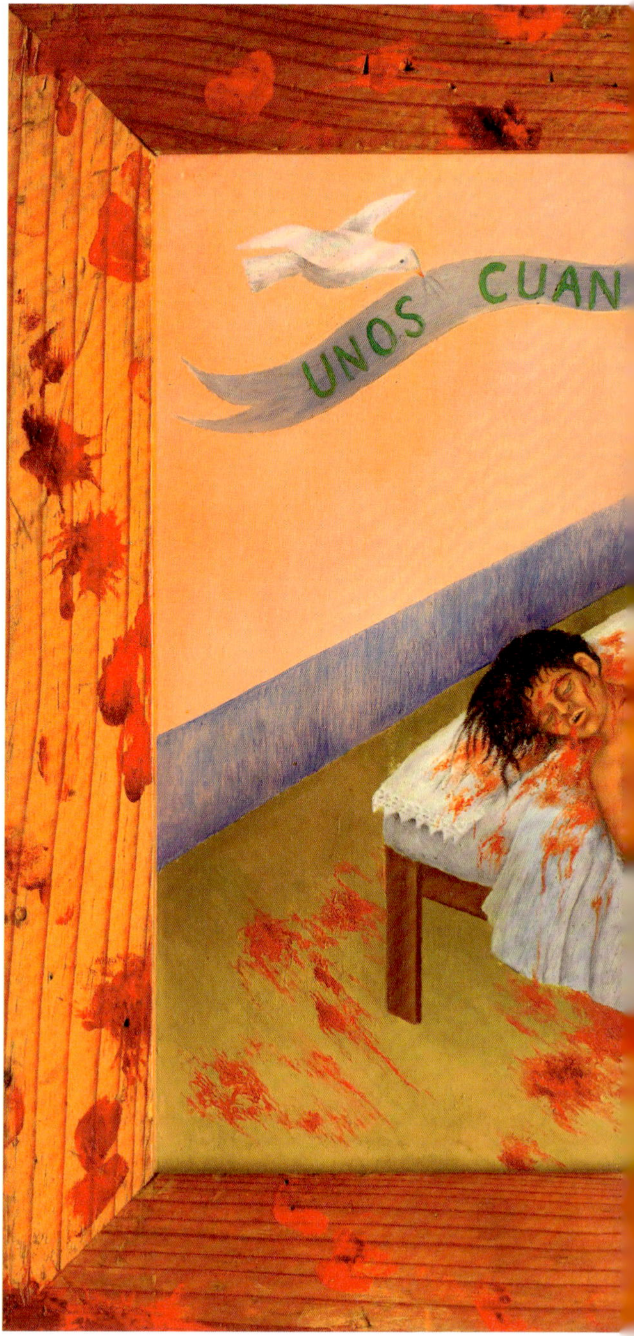

A Few Small Nips 1935
Oil paint on metal
30 × 40

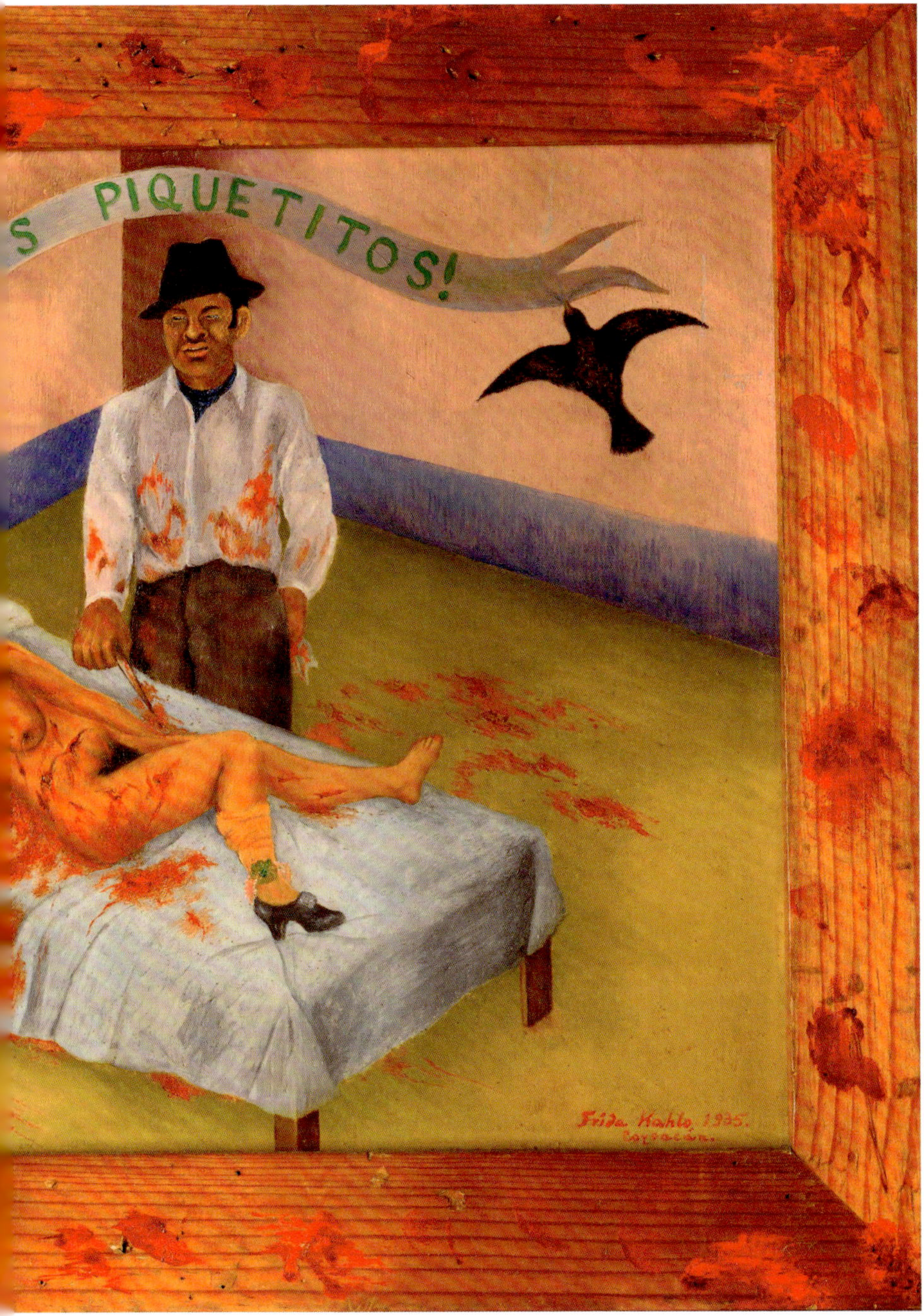
S PIQUETITOS!
Frida Kahlo 1935.

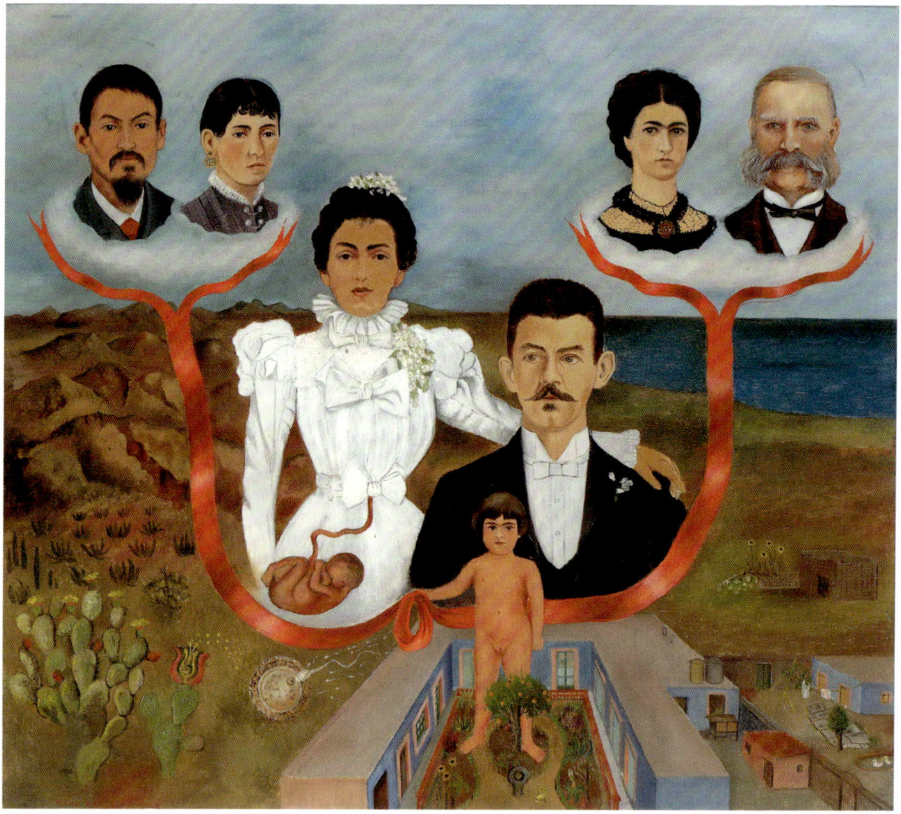

My Grandparents, My Parents, and I 1936
Oil paint and tempera on zinc
30.7 × 34.5

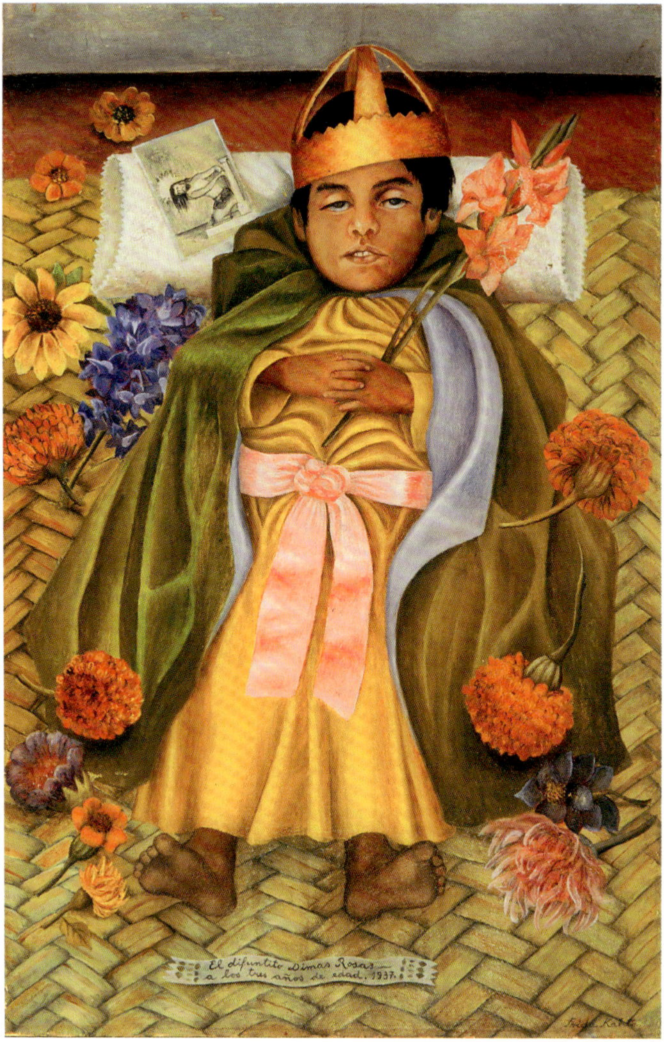

The Deceased Dimas Rosas
(at Three Years of Age) 1937
Oil paint on masonite
48 × 31.5

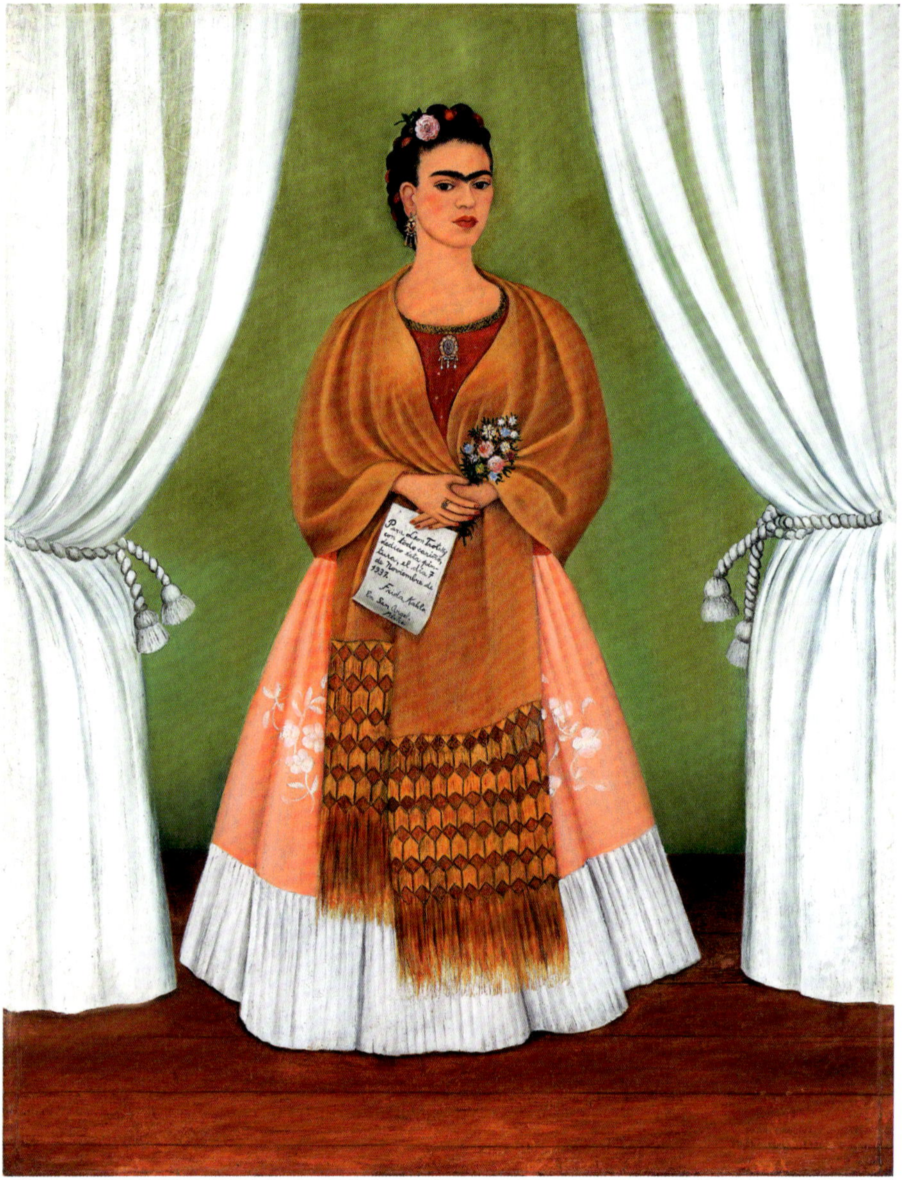

Self-Portrait Dedicated to Leon Trotsky 1937
Oil paint on masonite
76.2 × 61

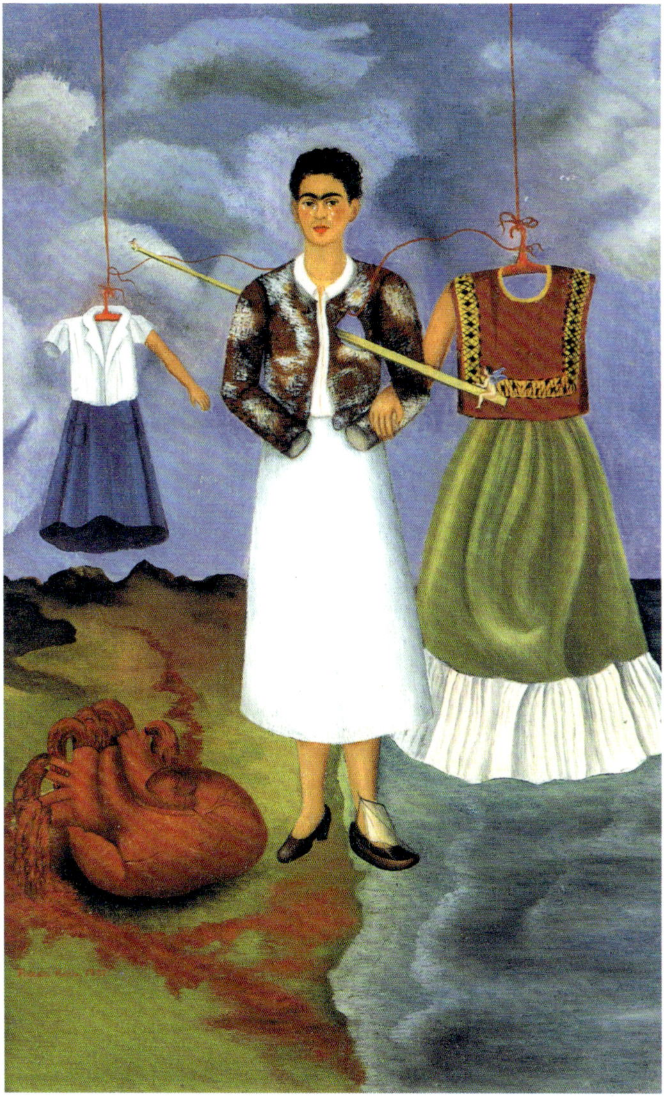

Memory (The Heart) 1937
Oil paint on metal
40 × 28

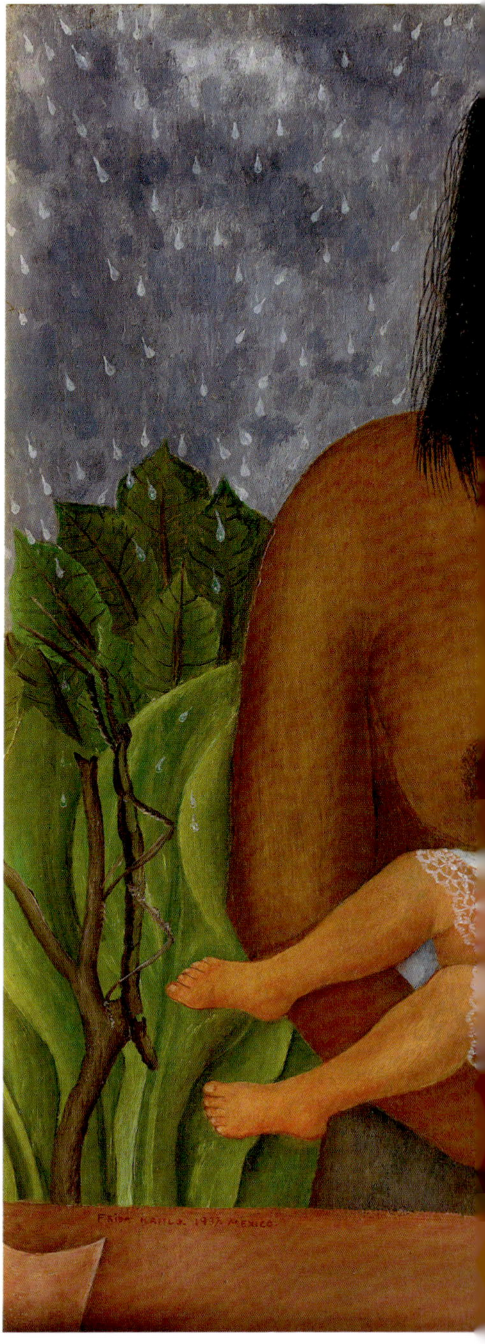

My Nurse and I 1937
Oil paint on metal
30.5 × 35

OVERLEAF
Fulang-Chang and I 1937
Two parts: oil paint on hardboard with painted mirror frame (added after 1939) and mirror with painted mirror frame (after 1939)
Framed painting, left 56.5 × 44.1 × 4.4 and framed mirror, right 64.1 × 48.3 × 4.4

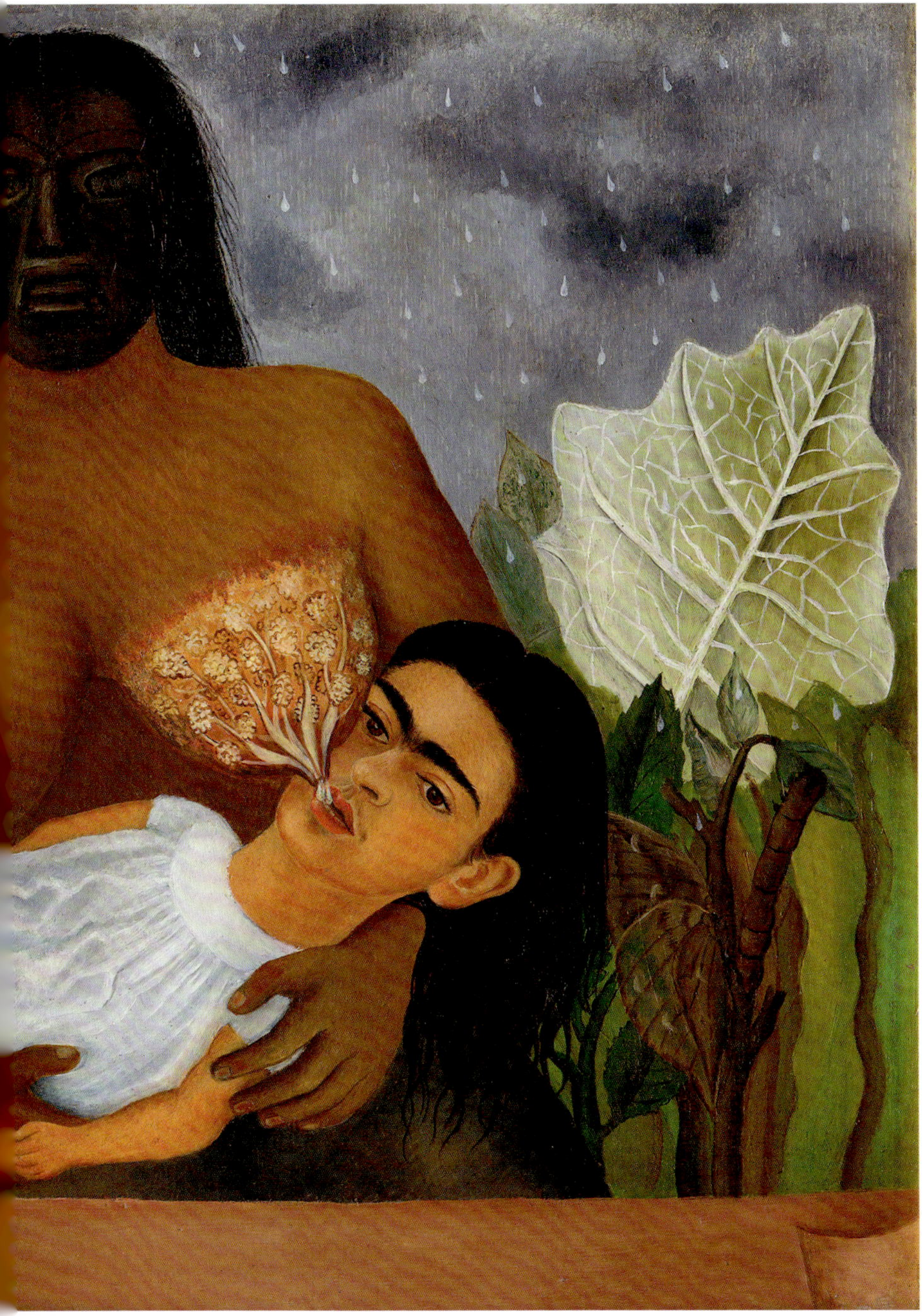

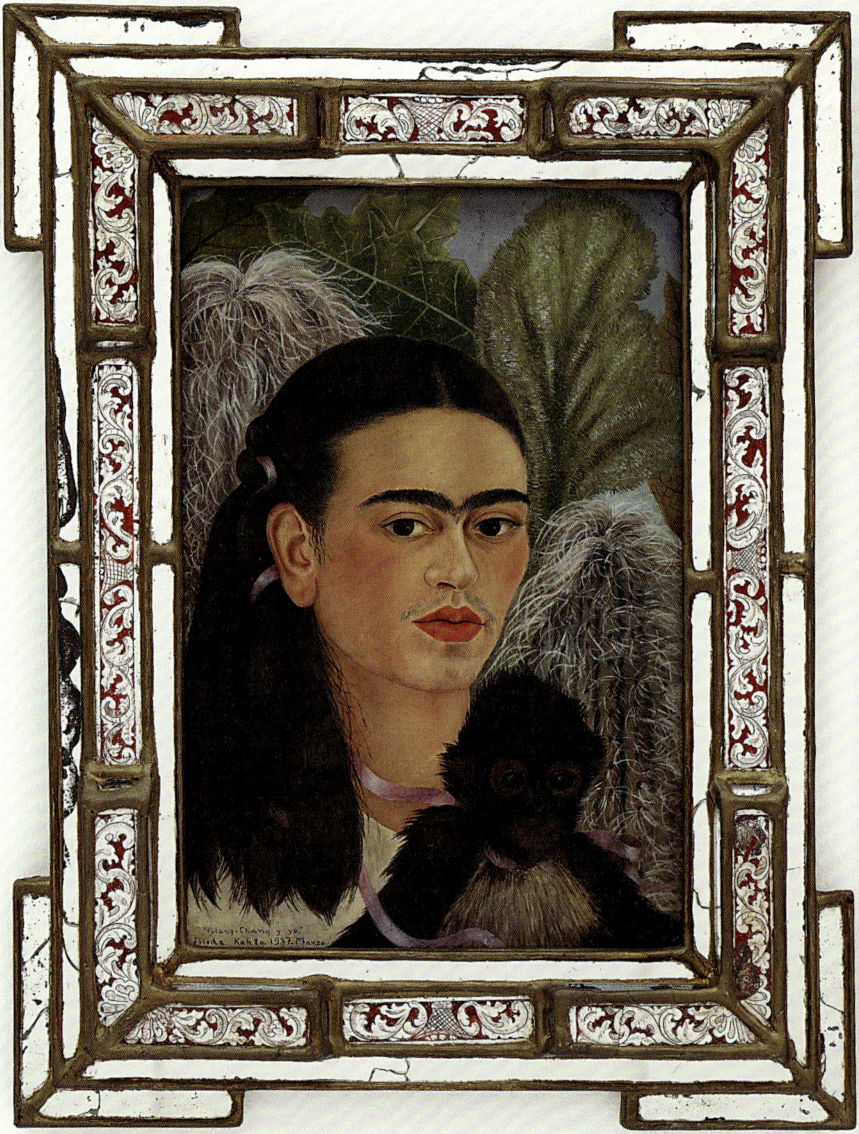
"Fulang-Chang y yo."
Frida Kahlo. 1937. Marzo.

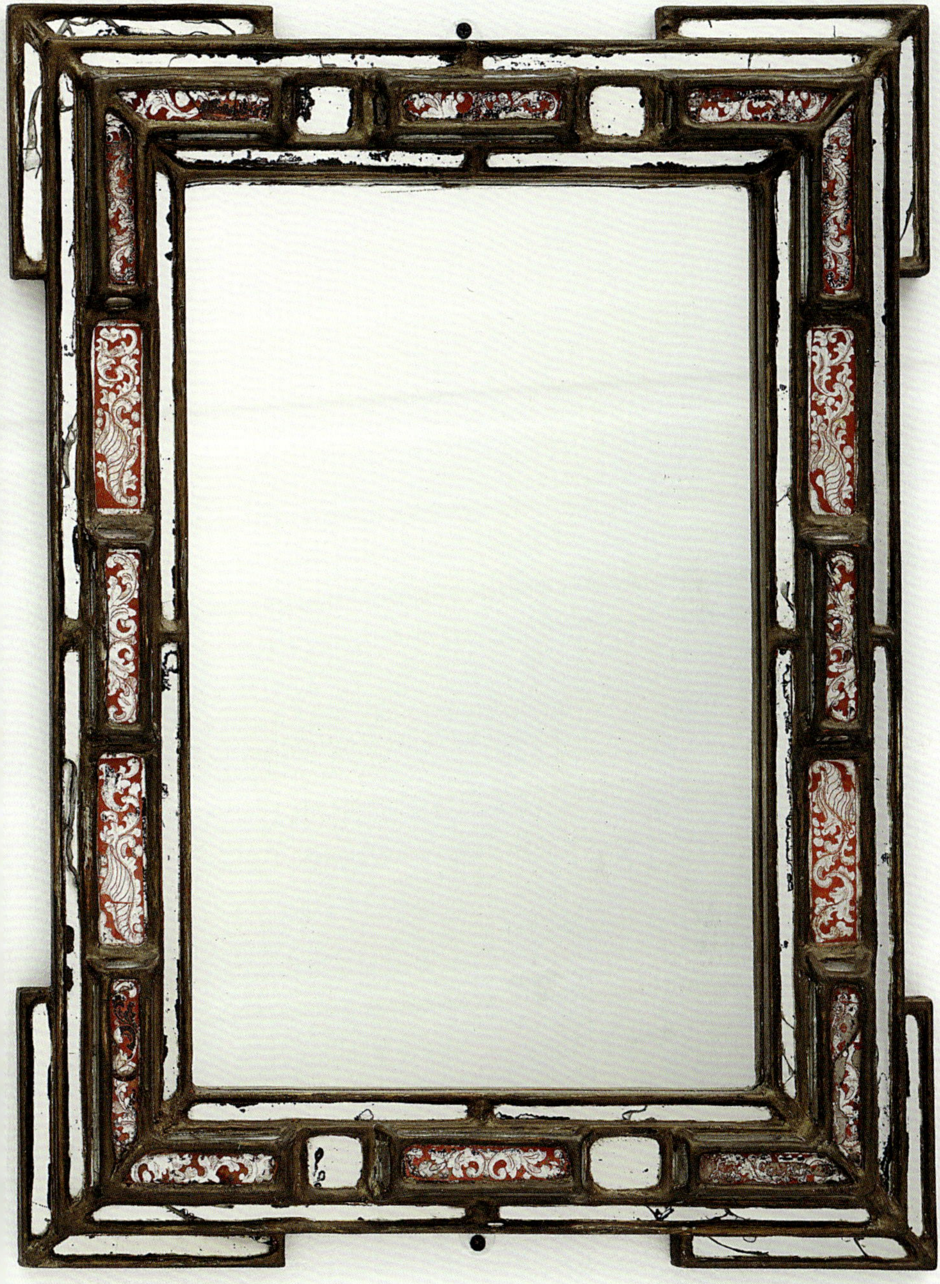

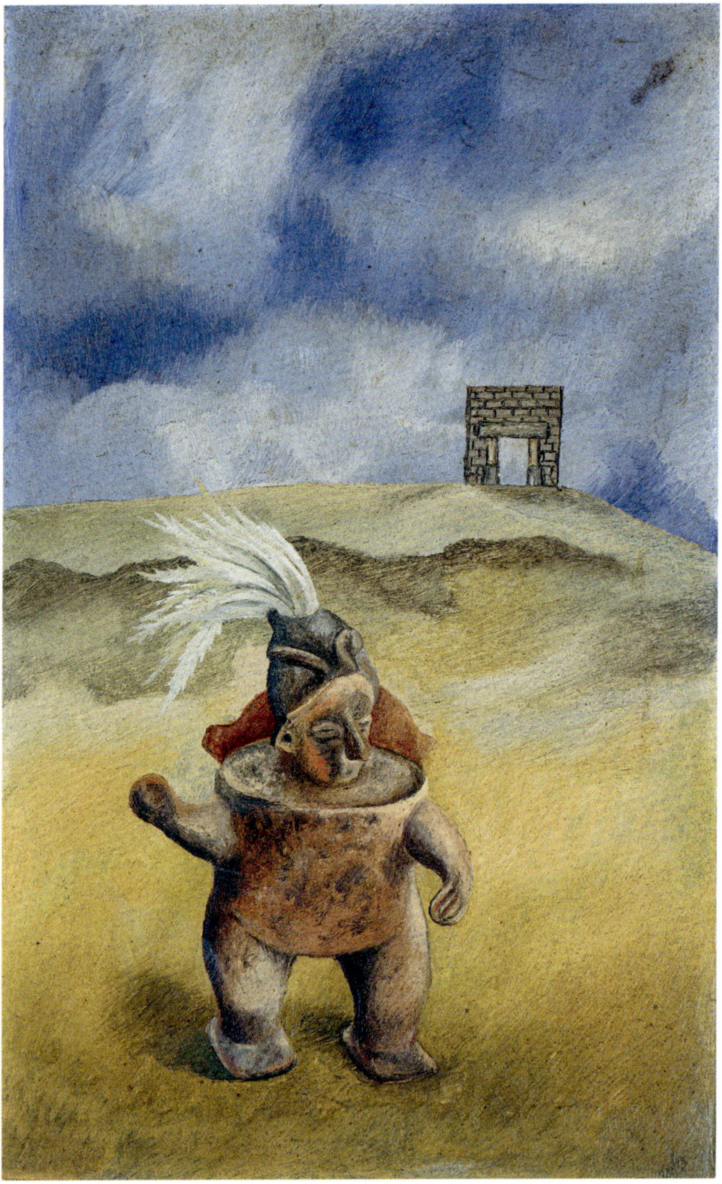

Survivor 1938
Oil paint on metal framed by artist in a handcrafted Oaxacan tin frame
45·5 × 37·5

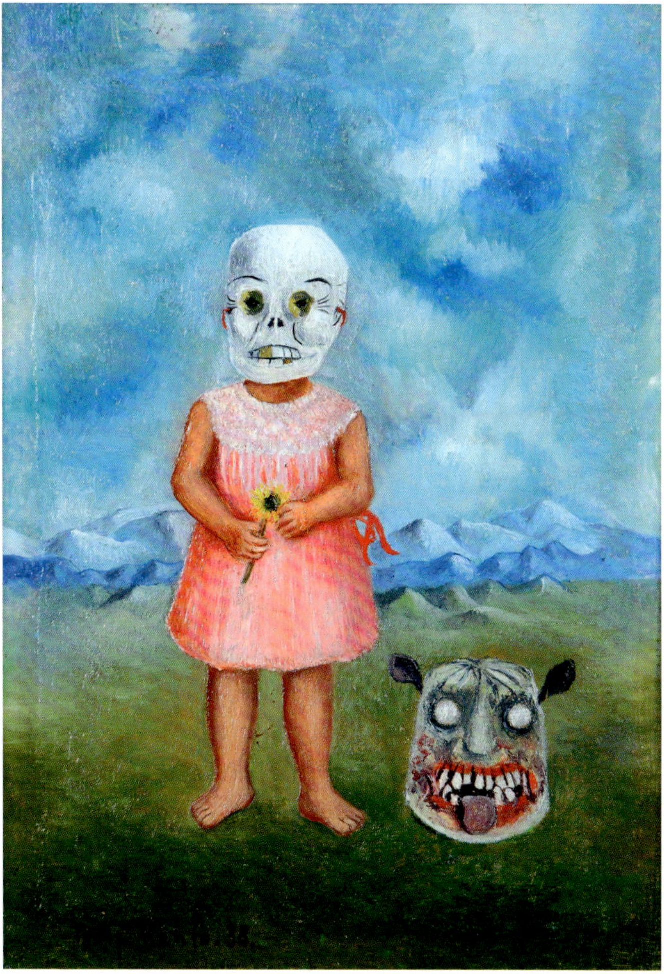

Girl with Death Mask 1938
Oil paint on tin plate
14.9 × 11

OVERLEAF
Four Inhabitants of Mexico
1938
Oil paint on metal
32.4 × 47.6

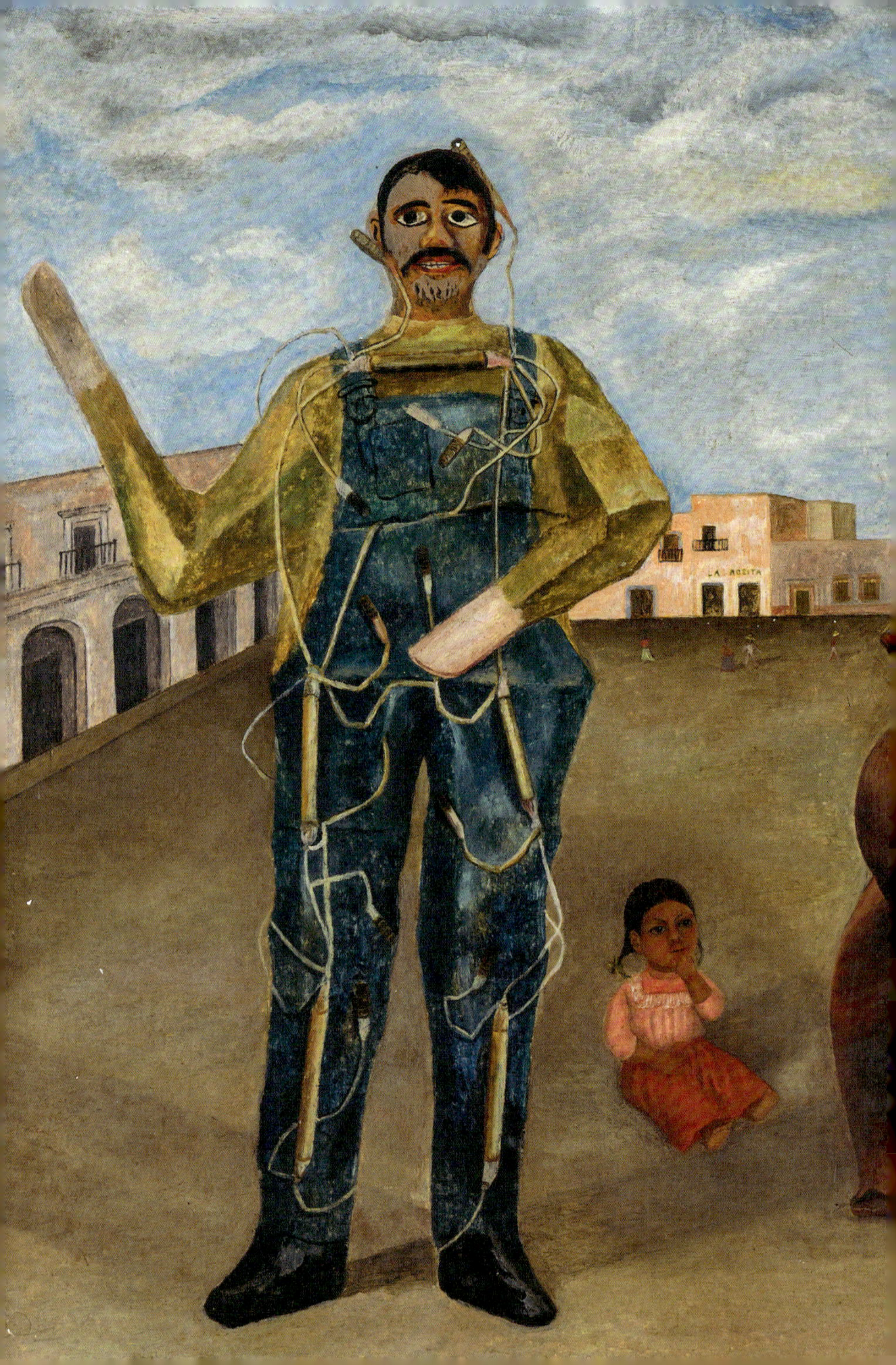
LA ROSITA

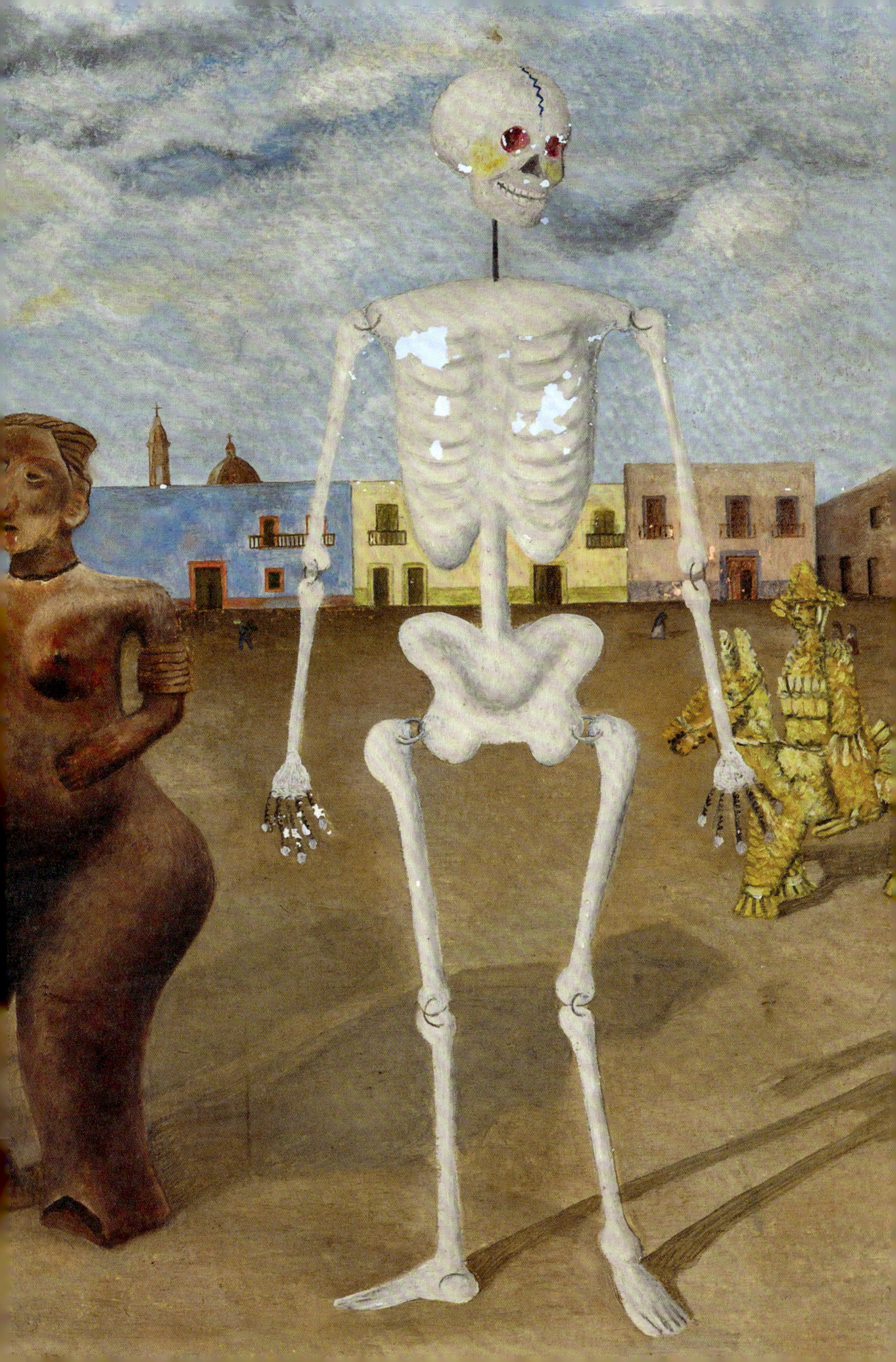

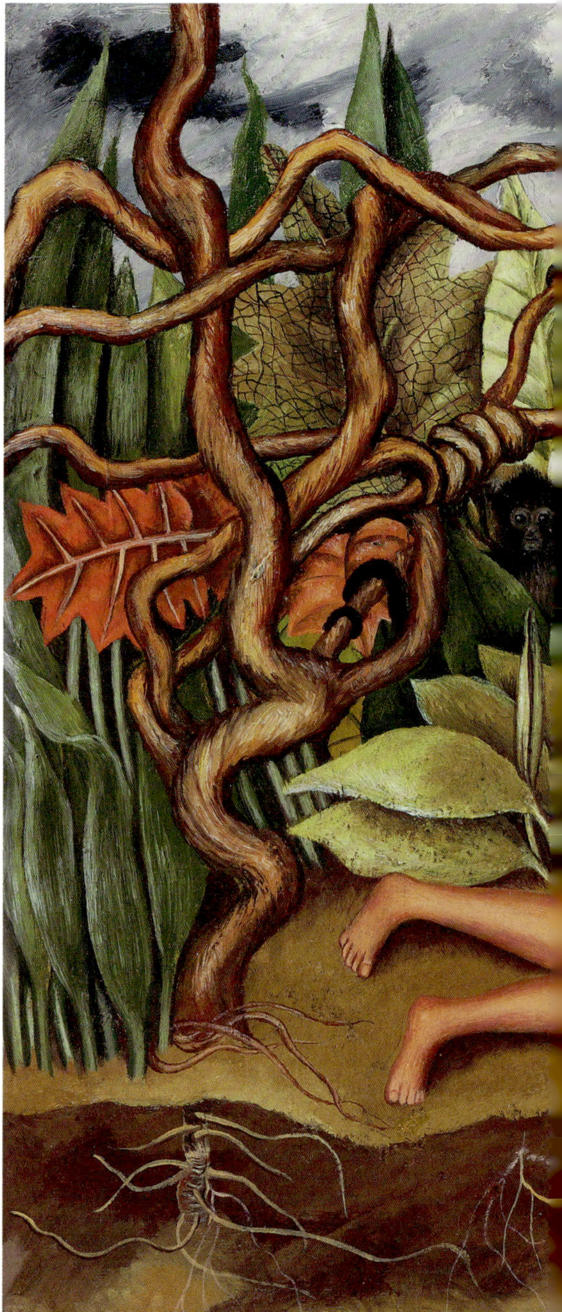

Two Nudes in a Forest 1939
Oil paint on metal
25.1 × 30.2

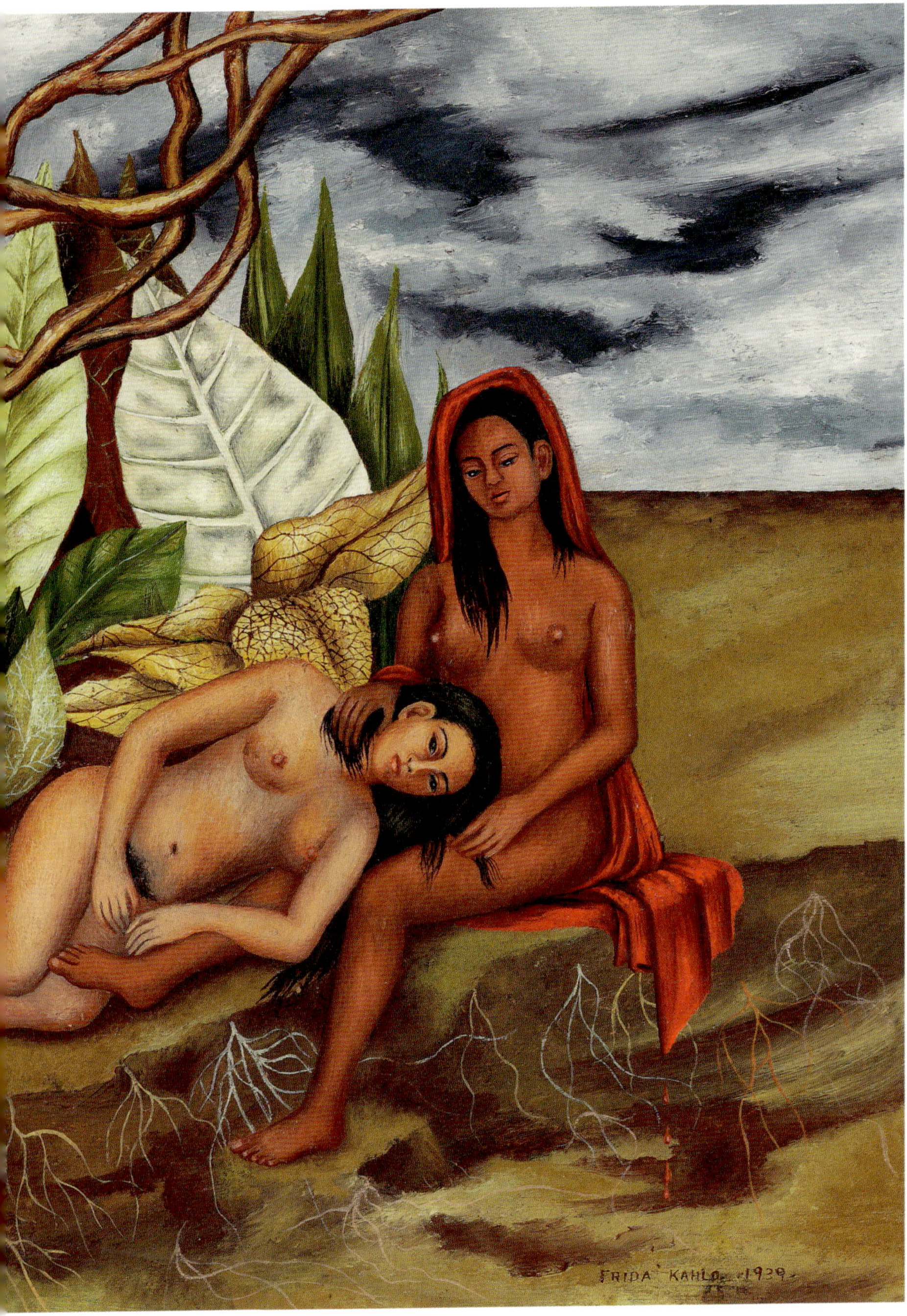
FRIDA KAHLO 1939

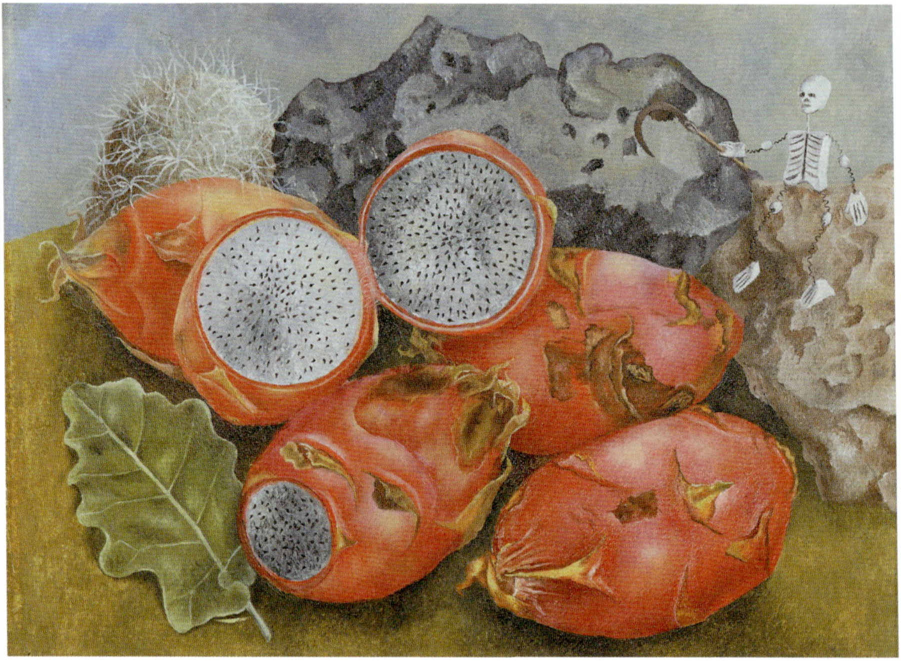

Pitahayas 1938
Oil paint on aluminium
25.4 × 35.6

The Frame 1938
Oil paint on aluminium
28.5 × 20.7

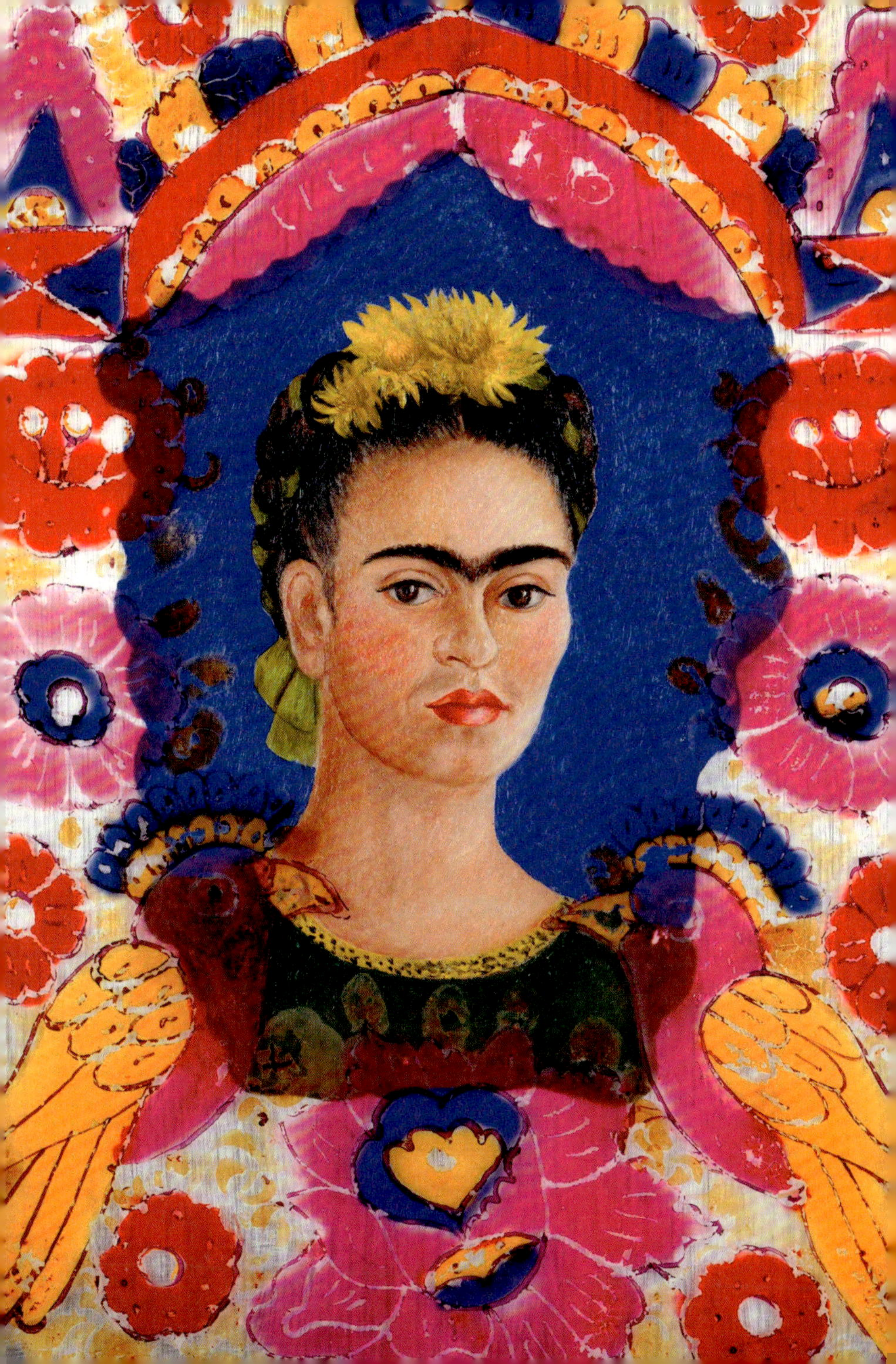

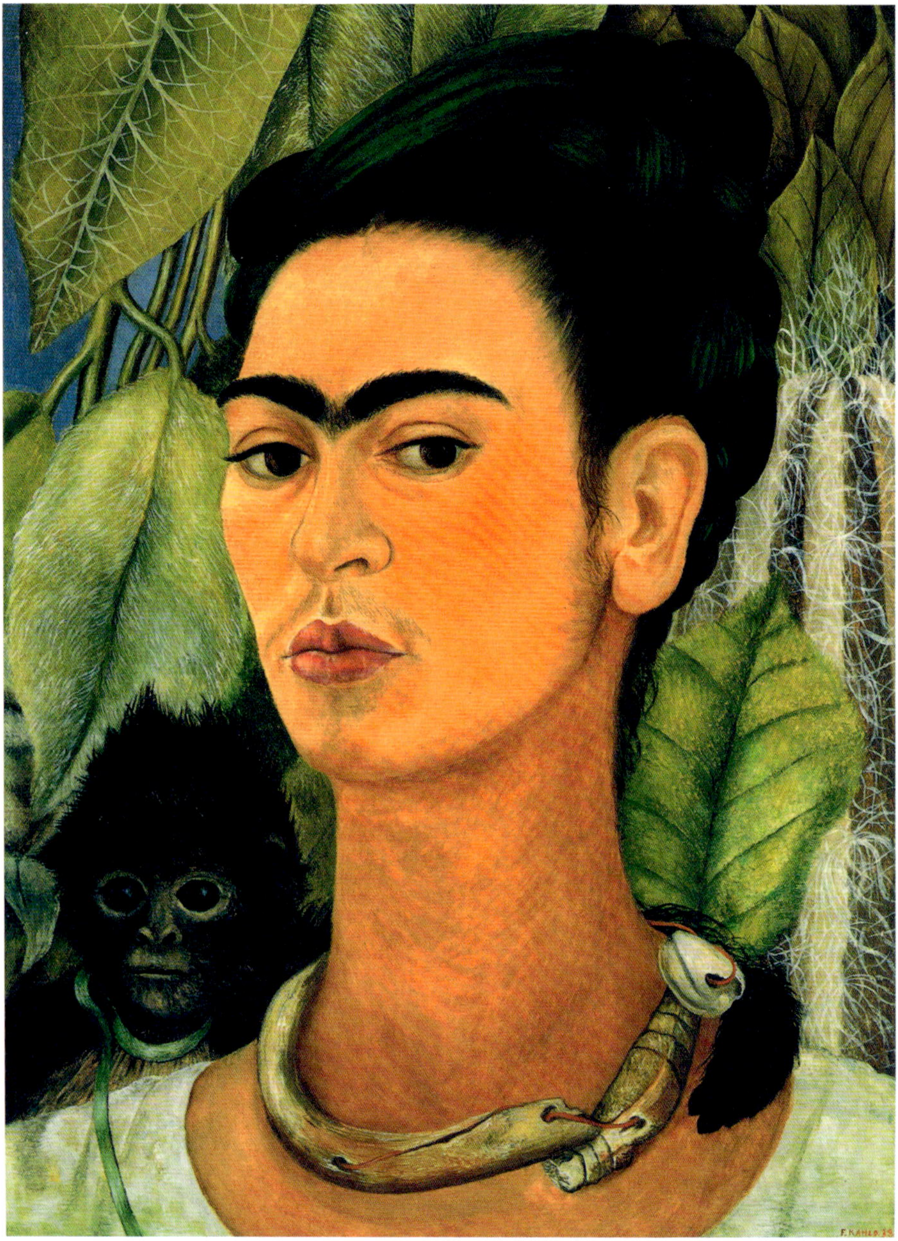

Self-Portrait with Monkey 1938
Oil paint on masonite
40.6 × 30.5

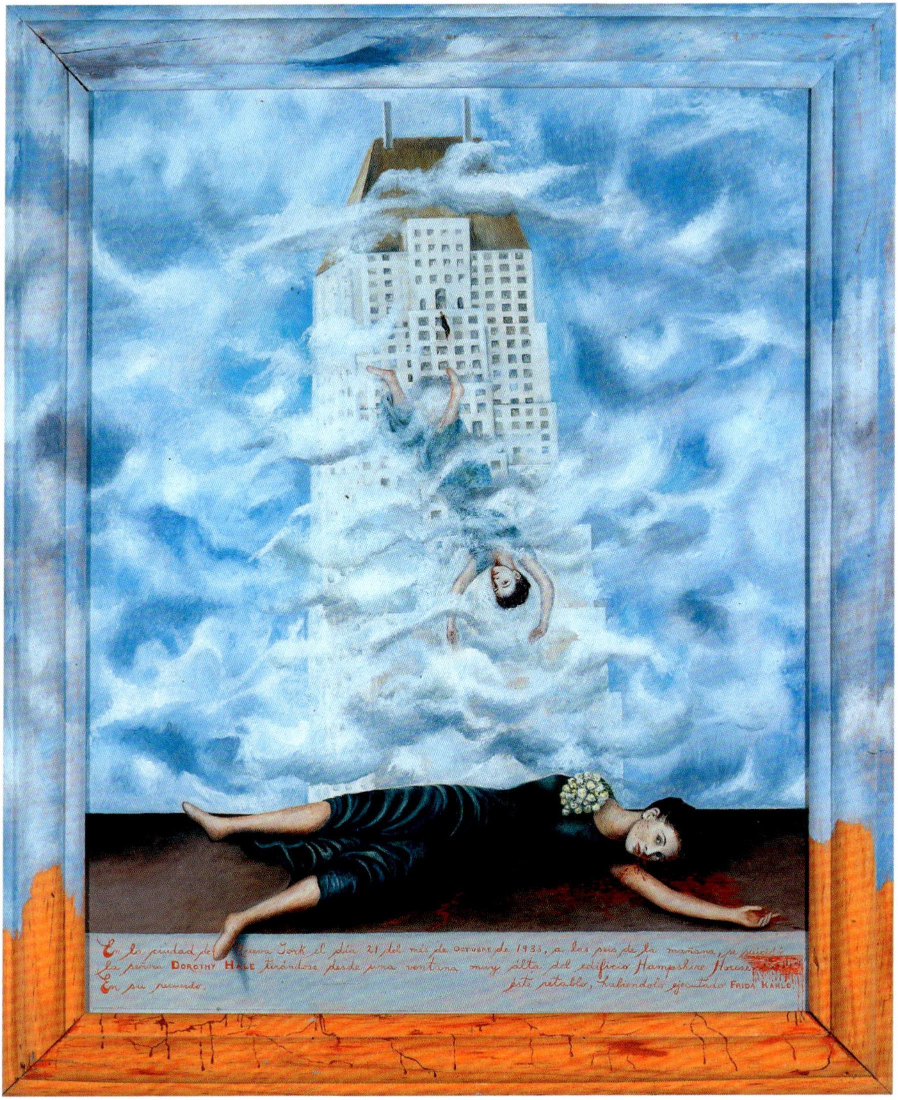

The Suicide of Dorothy Hale
1938–9
Oil paint on masonite
with painted frame
59·7 × 49·5

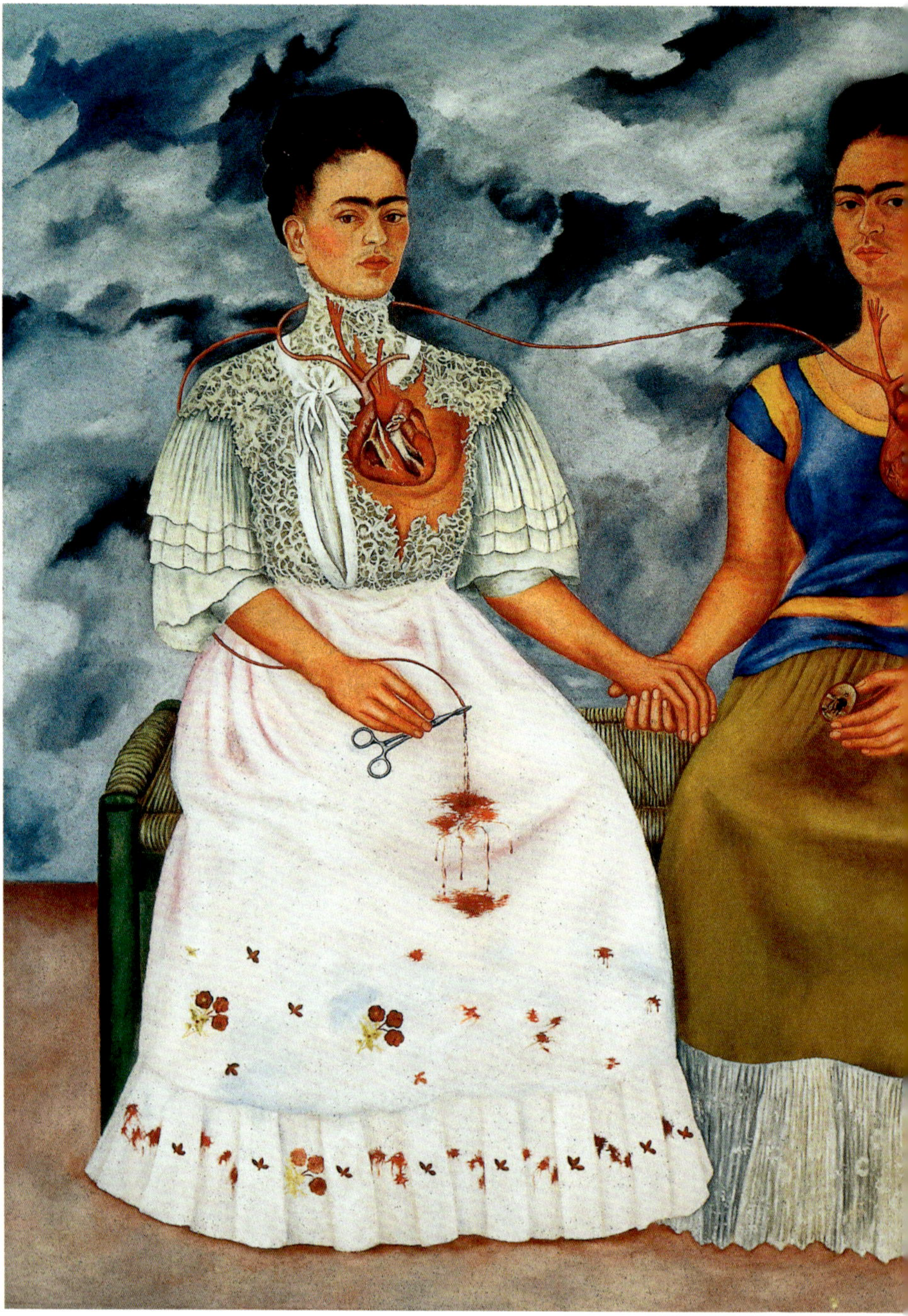

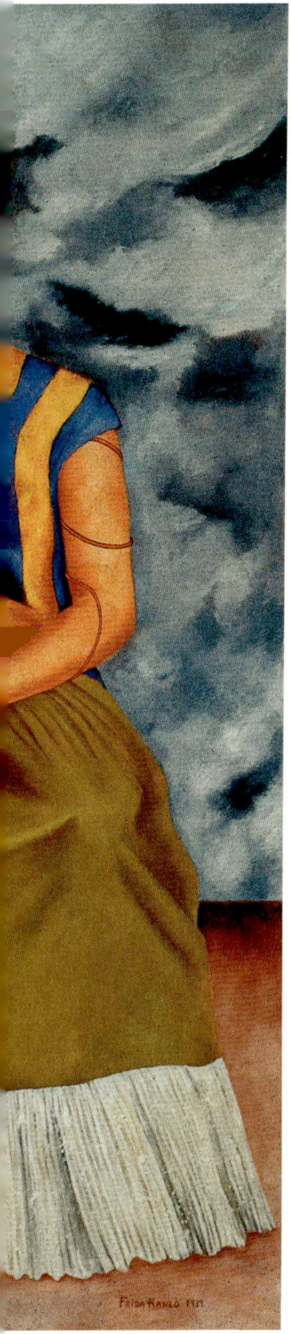

The Two Fridas 1939
Oil paint on canvas
173.5 × 173

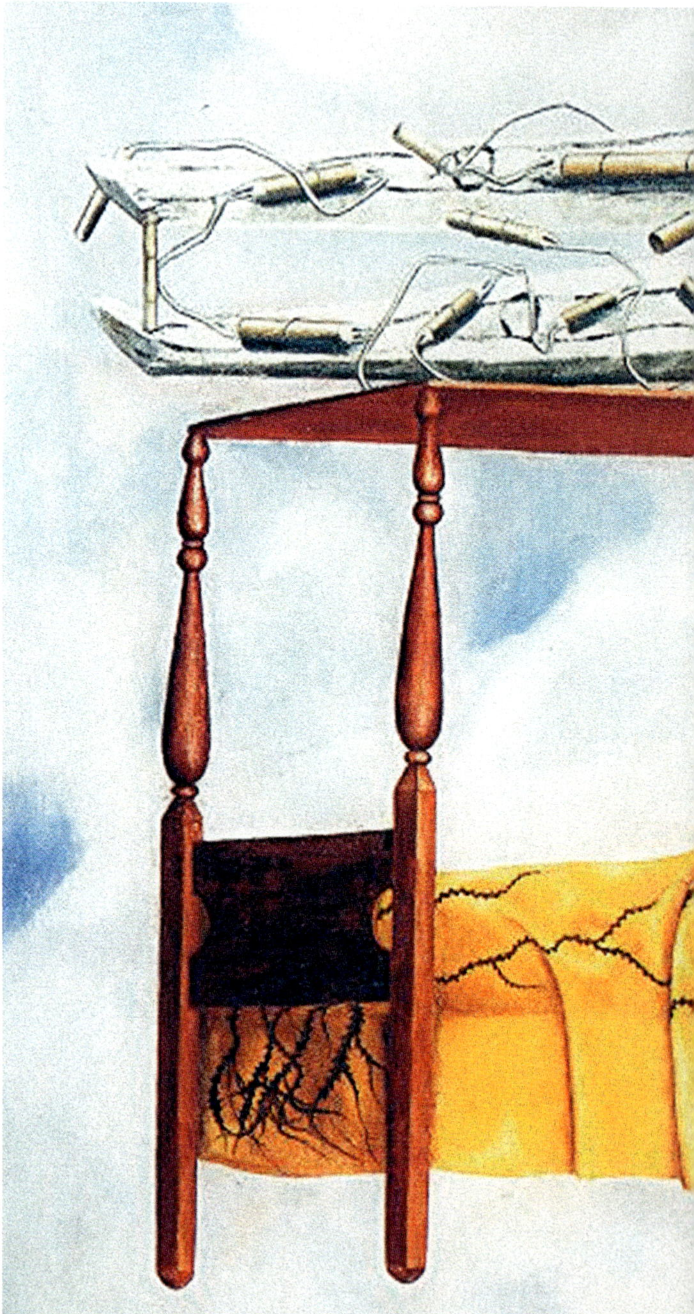

The Dream (The Bed) 1940
Oil paint on canvas
74 × 98.5

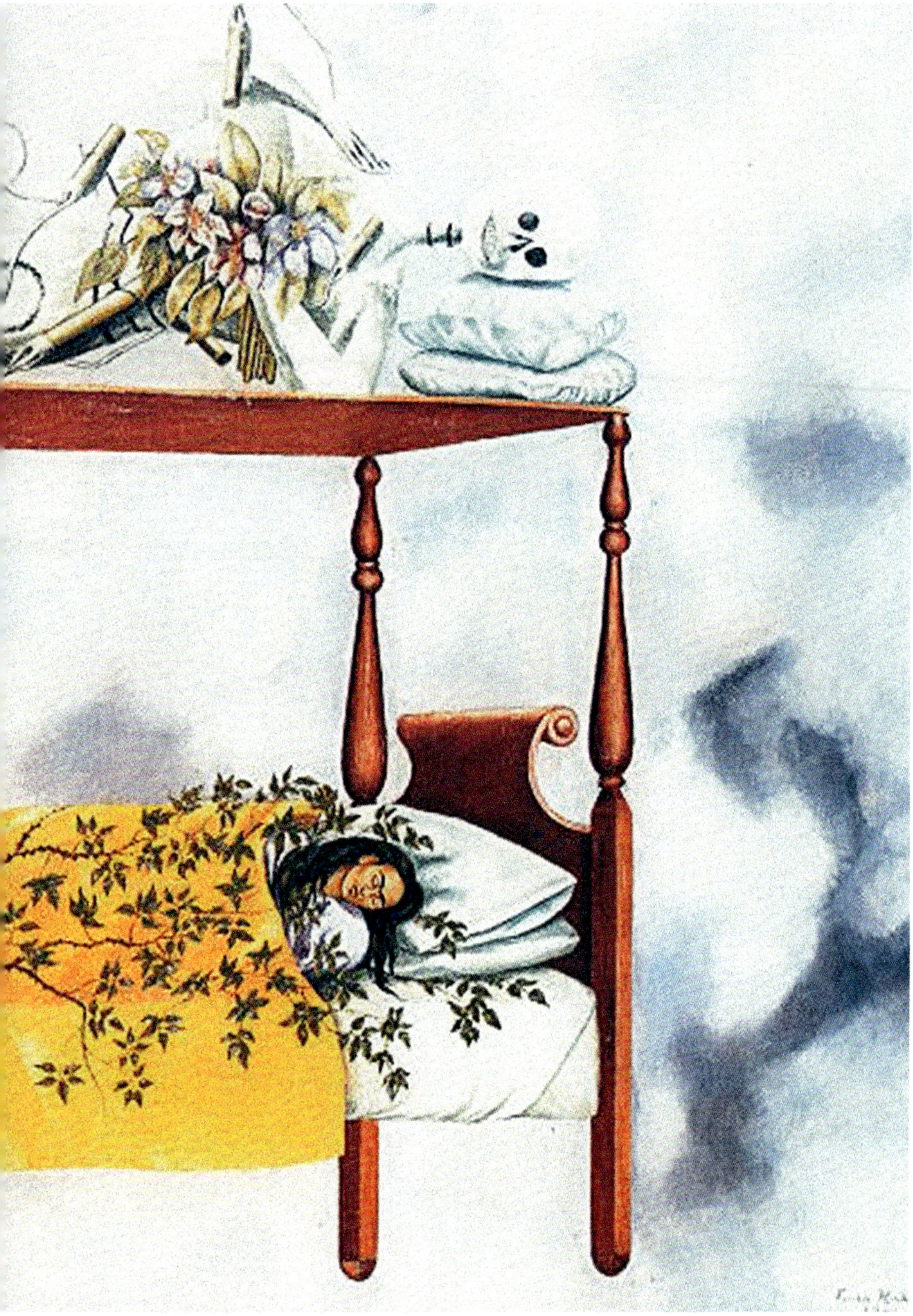

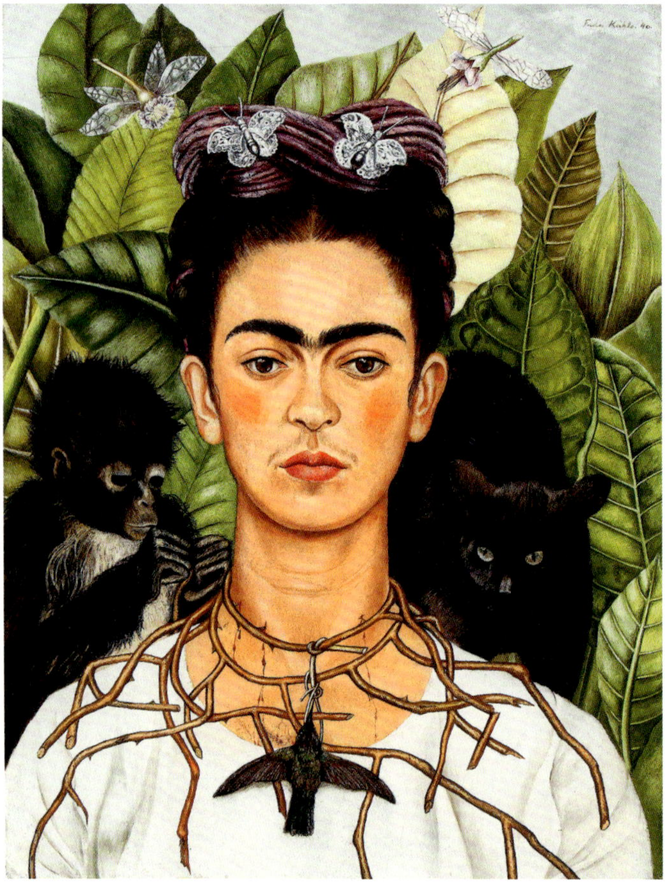

Self-Portrait with Thorn Necklace and Hummingbird
1940
Oil paint on canvas
63.5 × 49.5

Self-Portrait Dedicated to Dr Eloesser 1940
Oil paint on masonite
59.5 × 40

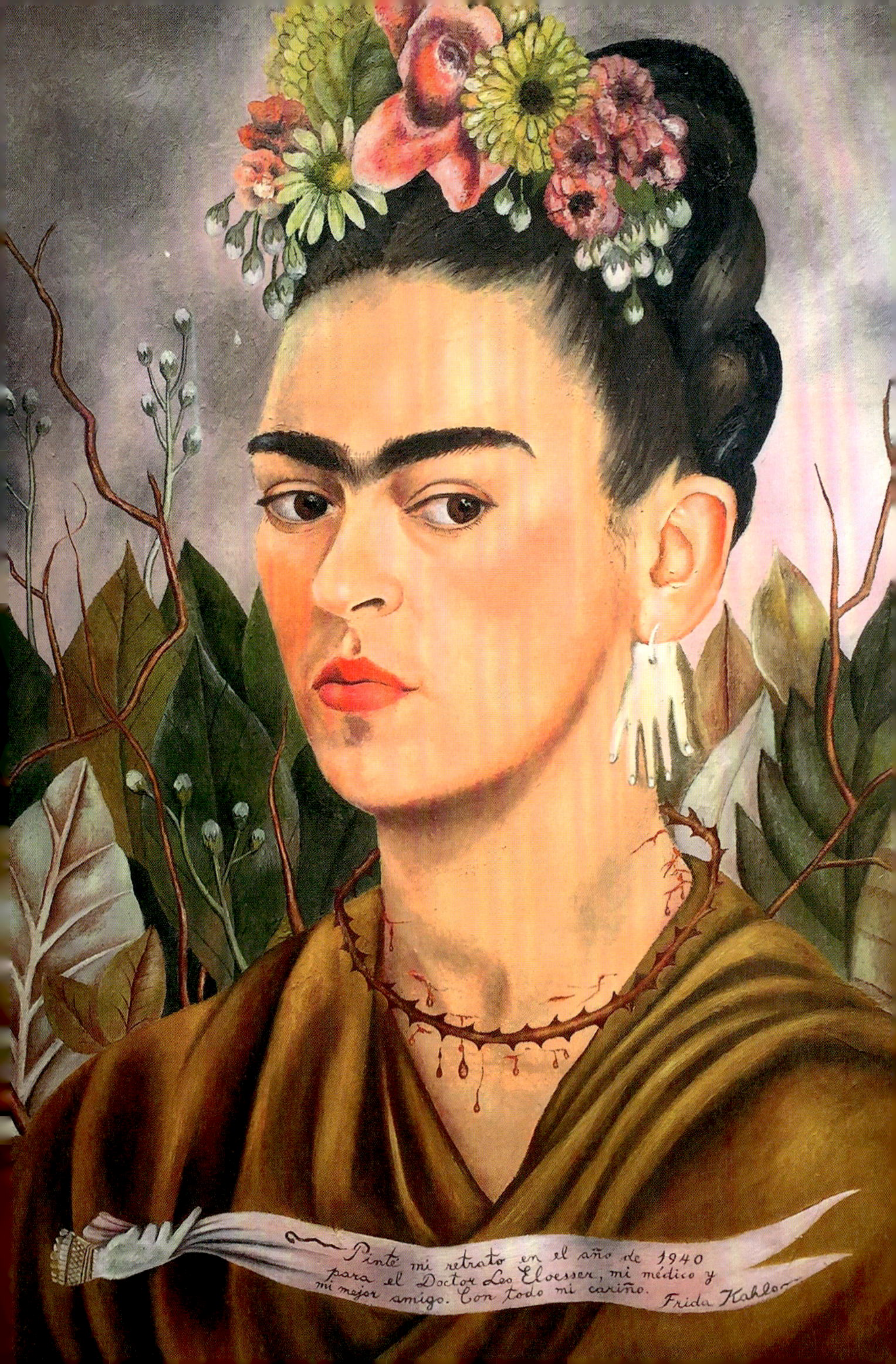
Pinté mi retrato en el año de 1940
para el Doctor Leo Eloesser, mi médico y
mi mejor amigo. Con todo mi cariño.
Frida Kahlo

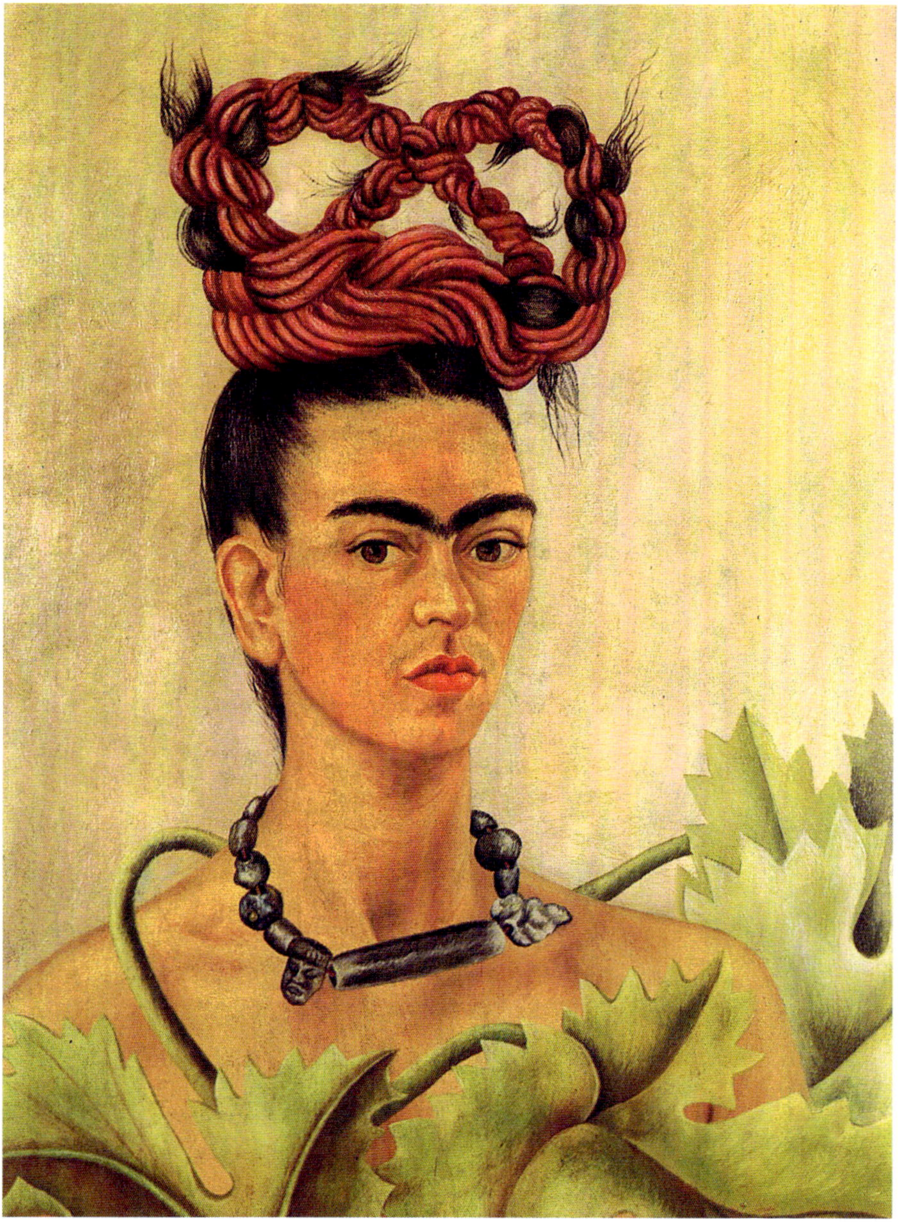

Self-Portrait with Braid 1941
Oil paint on masonite
51 × 38.5

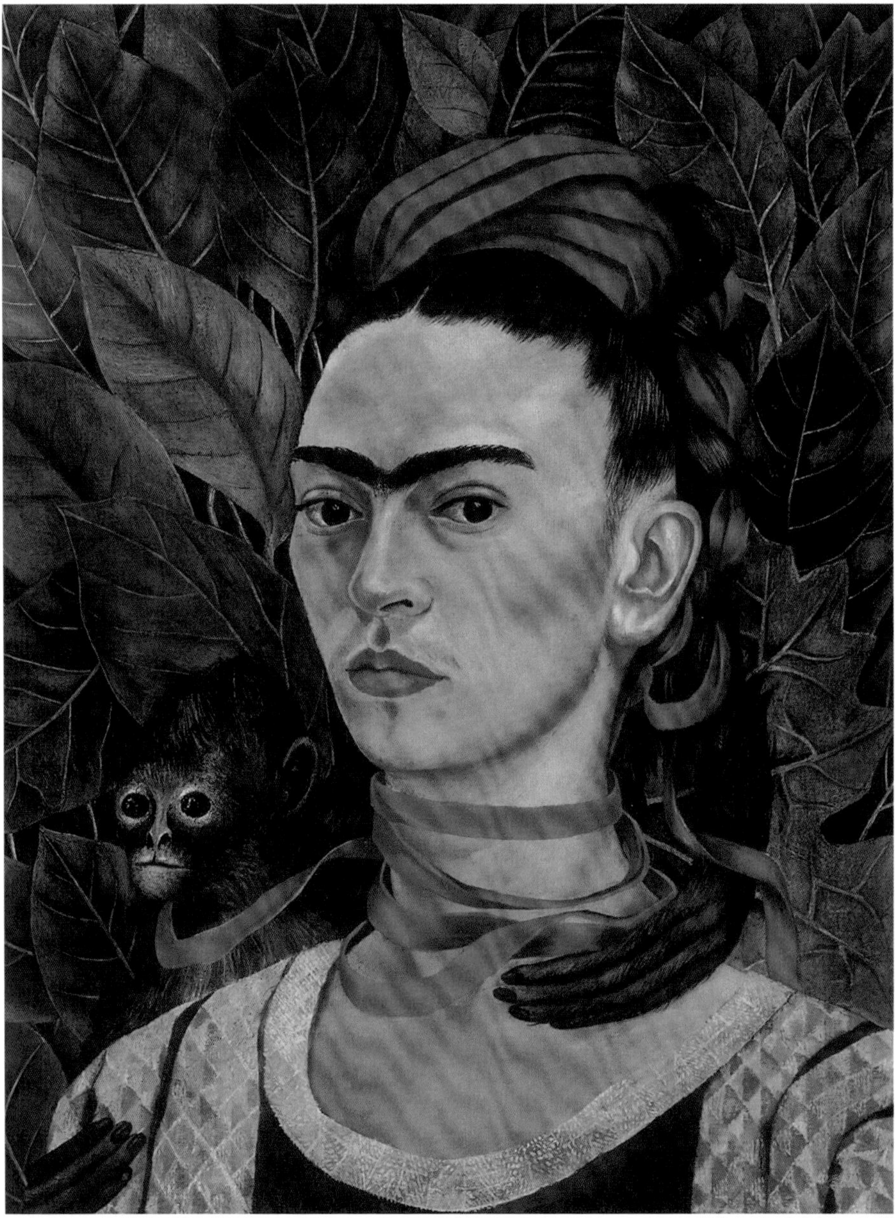

Self-Portrait with Monkey 1940
Oil paint on masonite
55.2 × 43.5

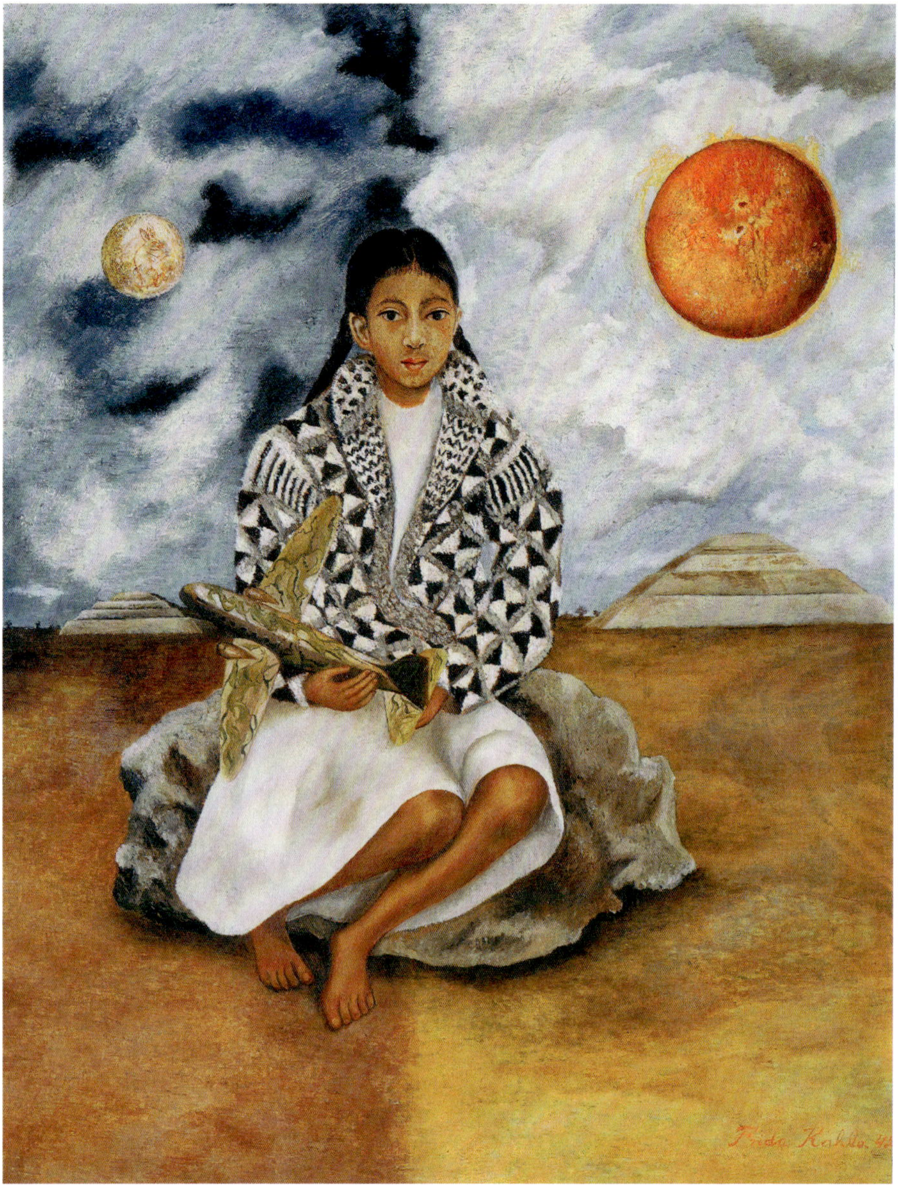

Portrait of Lucha Maria, A Girl from Tehuacán (Sun and Moon) 1942
Oil paint on masonite
54.6 × 43.2

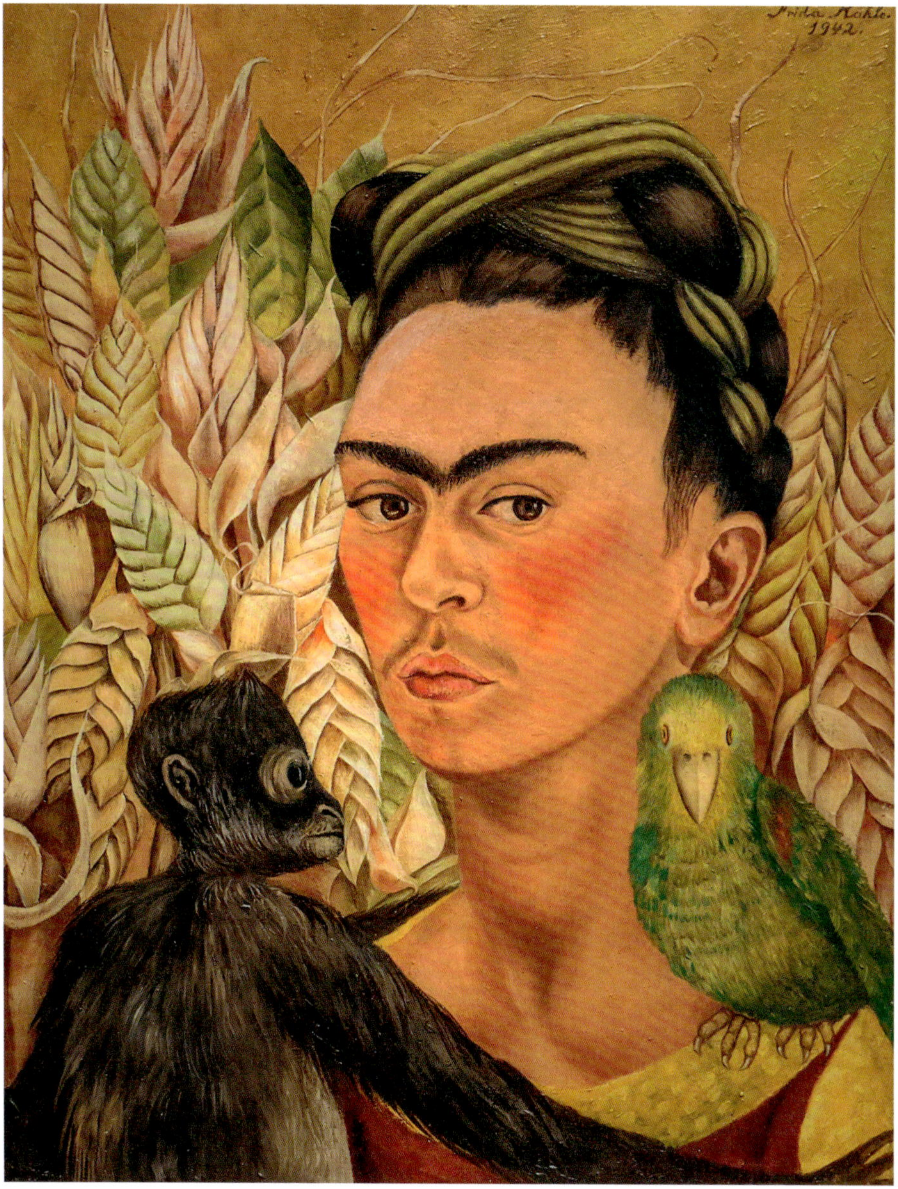

Self-Portrait with Monkey and Parrot 1942
Oil paint on masonite
54.6 × 43.2

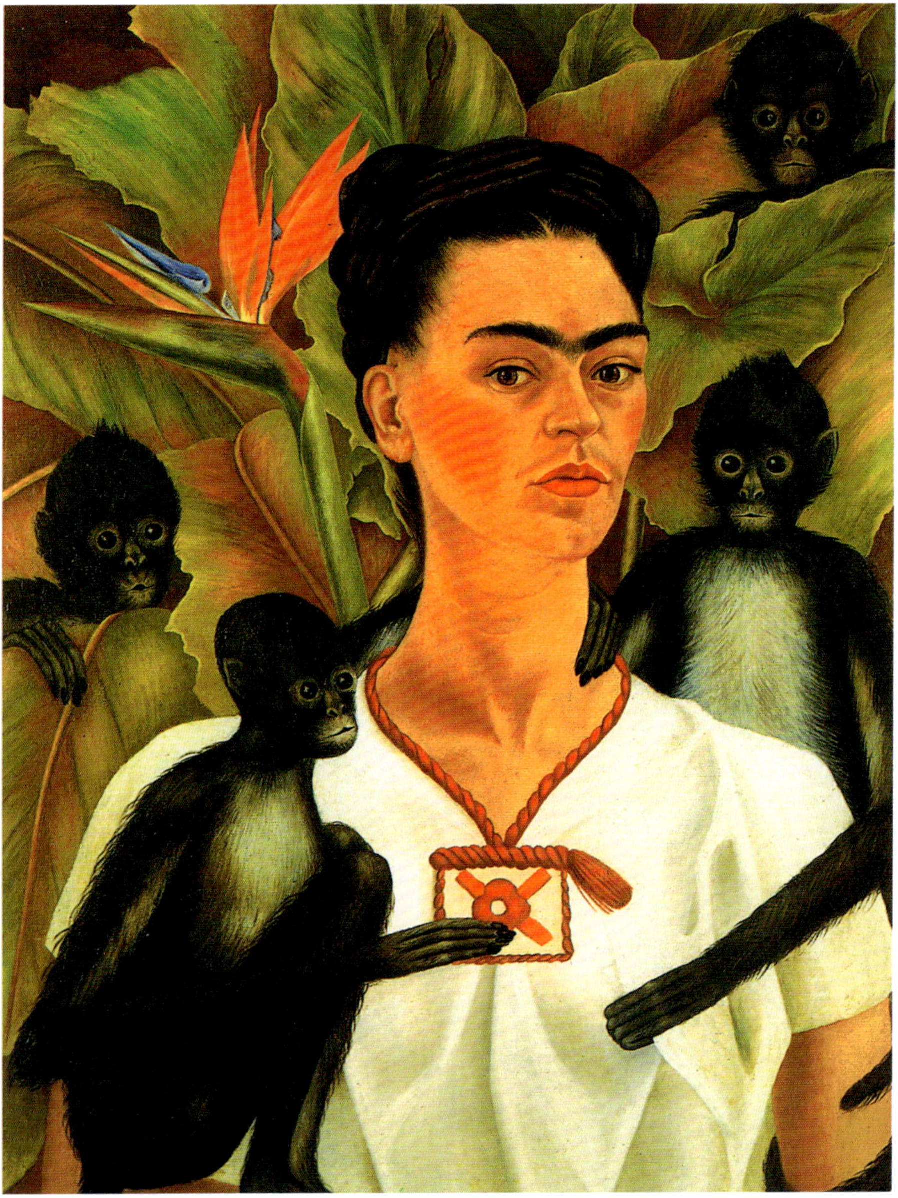

Self-Portrait with Monkeys
1943
Oil paint on canvas
81.5 × 63

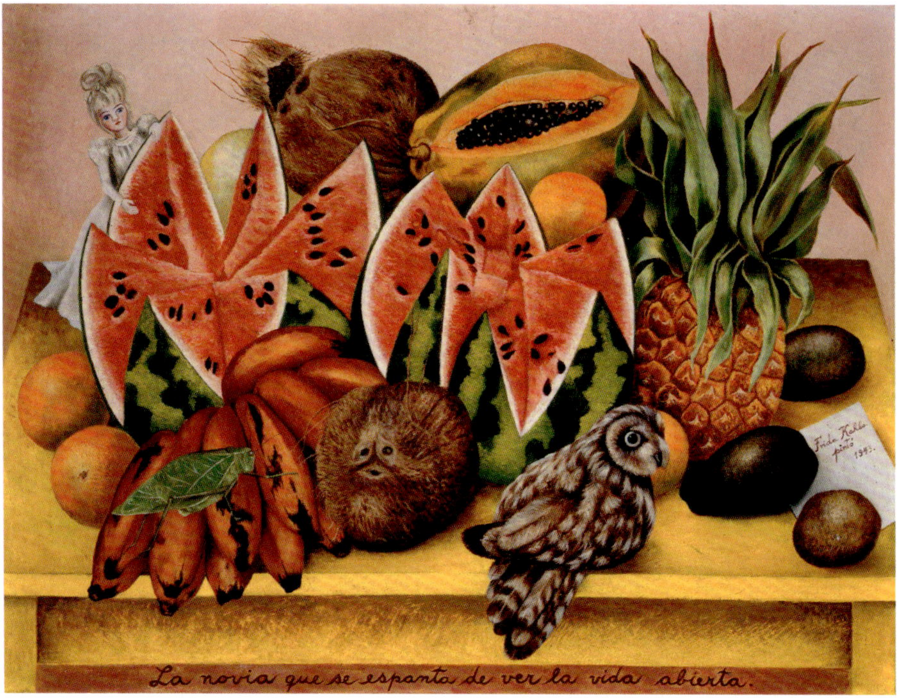

The Bride Frightened at Seeing Life Opened 1943
Oil paint on canvas
63 × 81.5

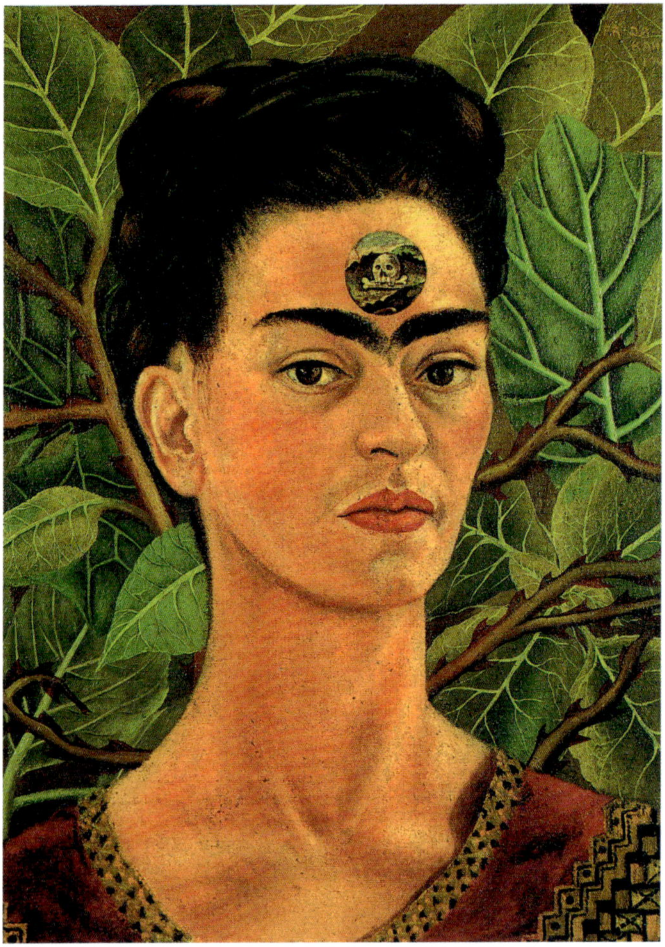

Thinking About Death 1943
Oil paint on masonite
44.5 × 36.2

Flower of Life 1943
Oil paint on masonite
27.8 × 19.7

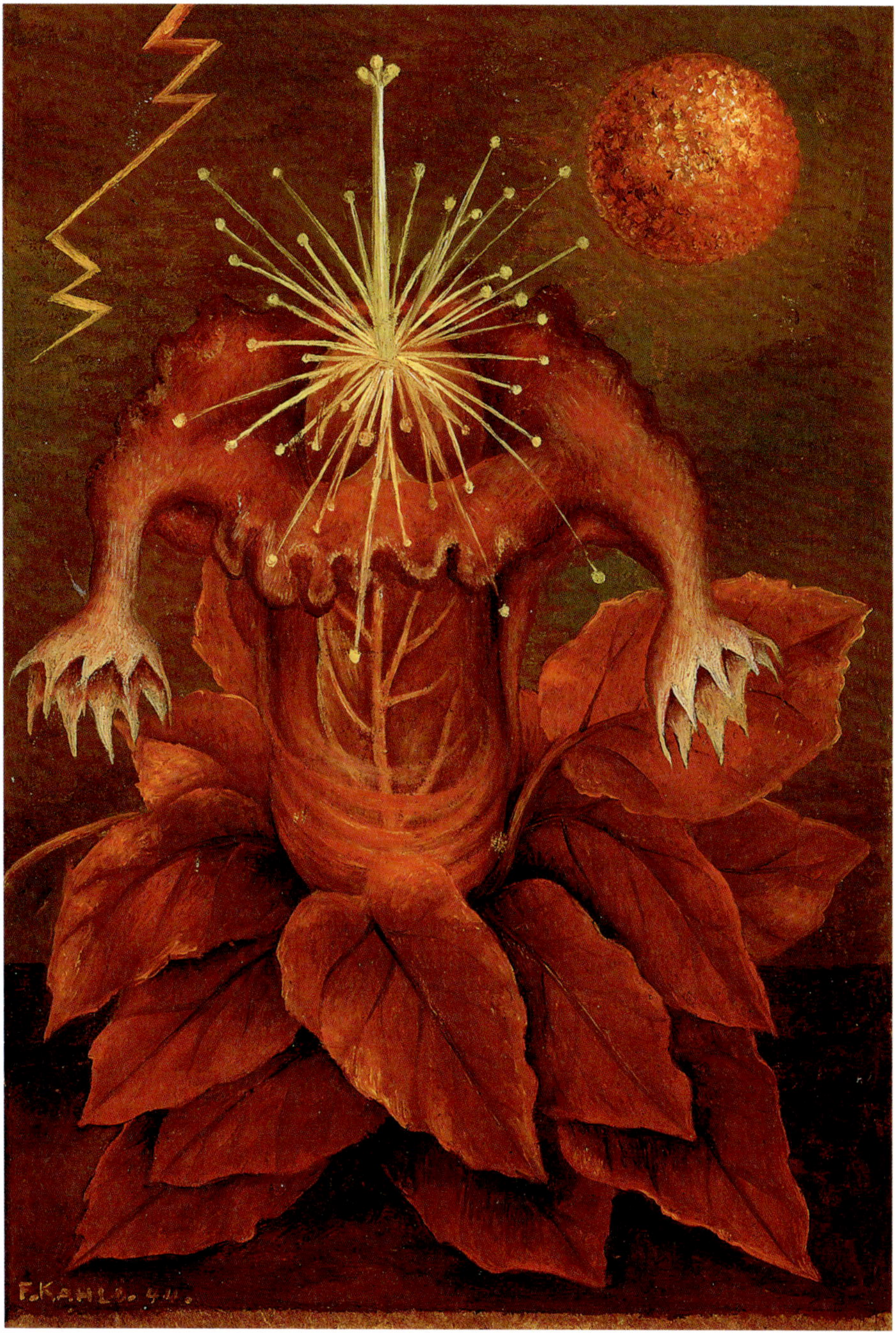
F.KAHLO. 44.

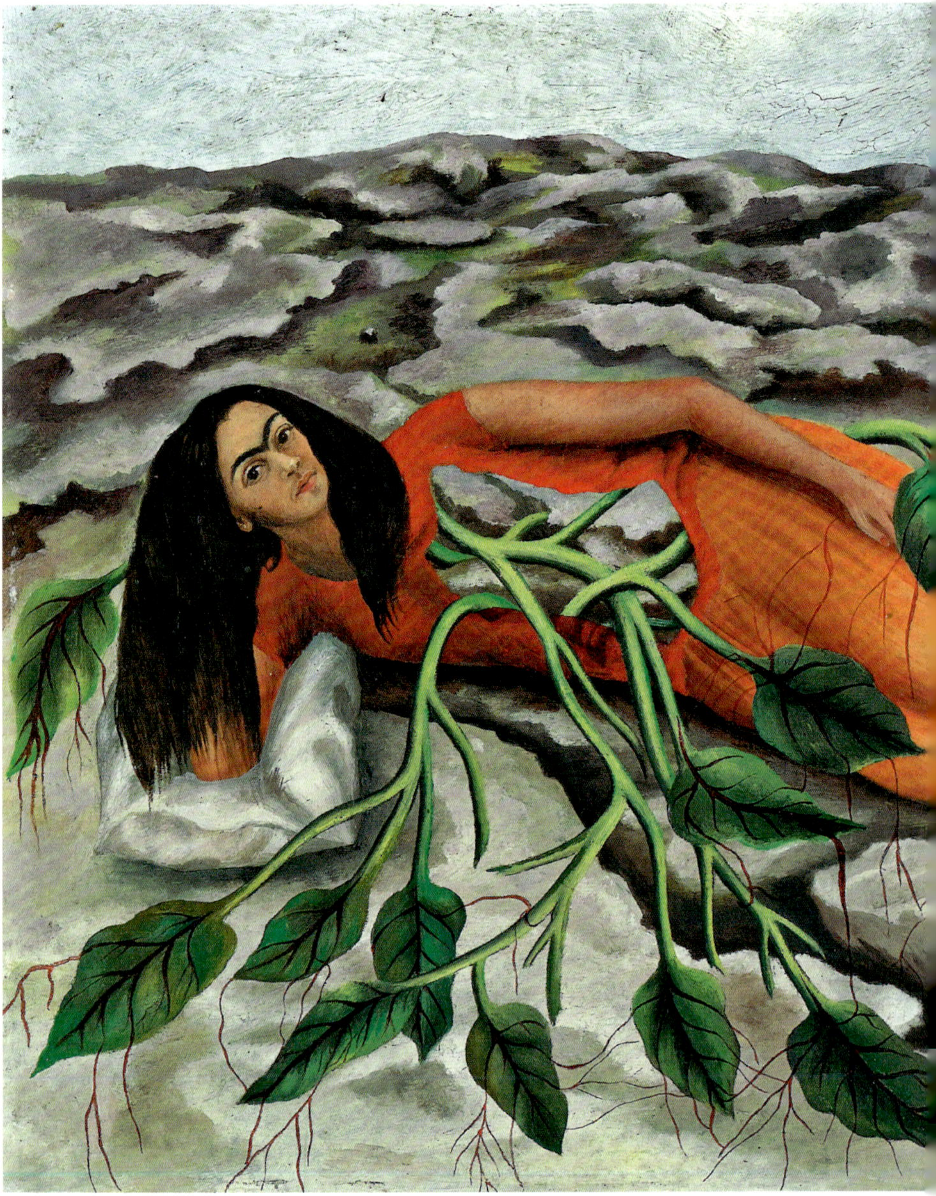

Roots 1943
Oil paint on metal
30.5 × 49.

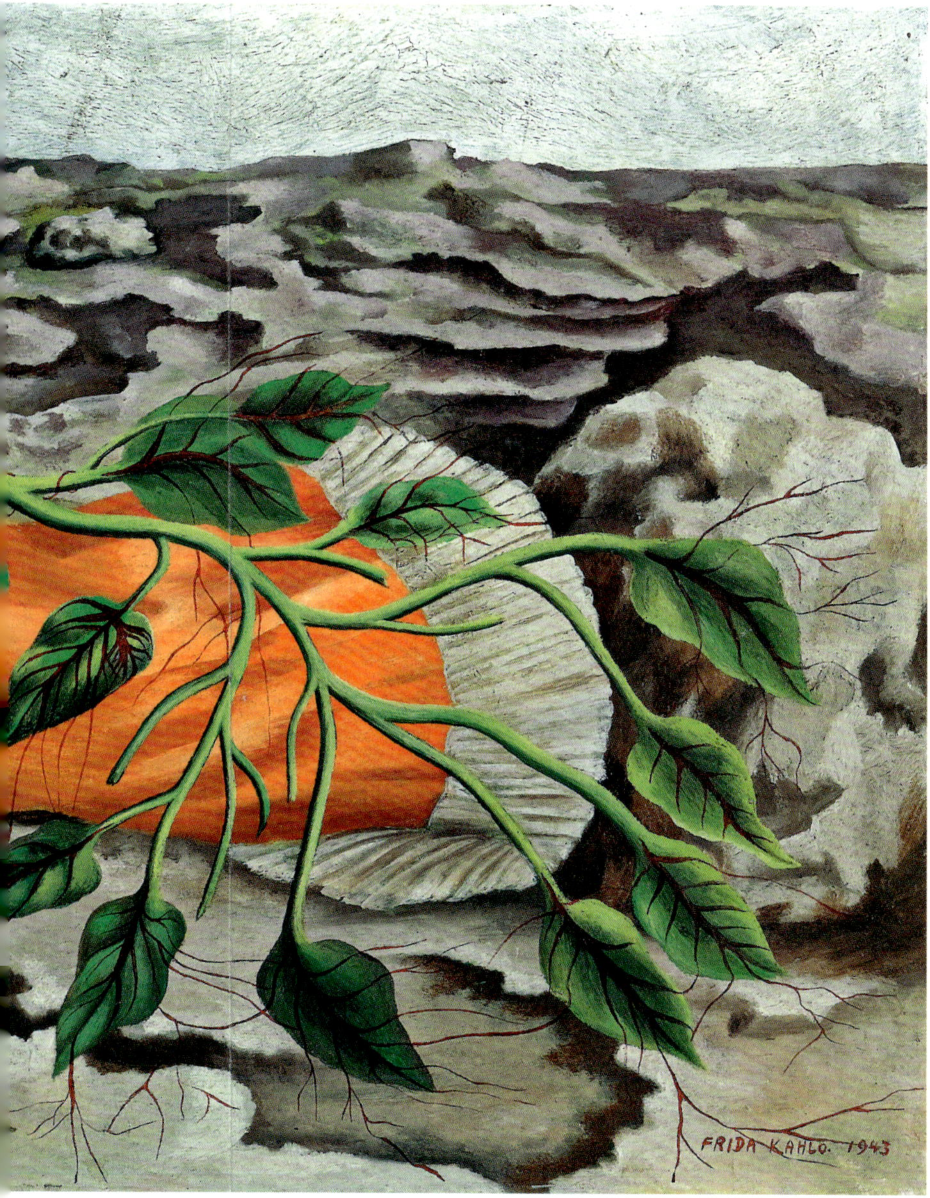
FRIDA KAHLO. 1943

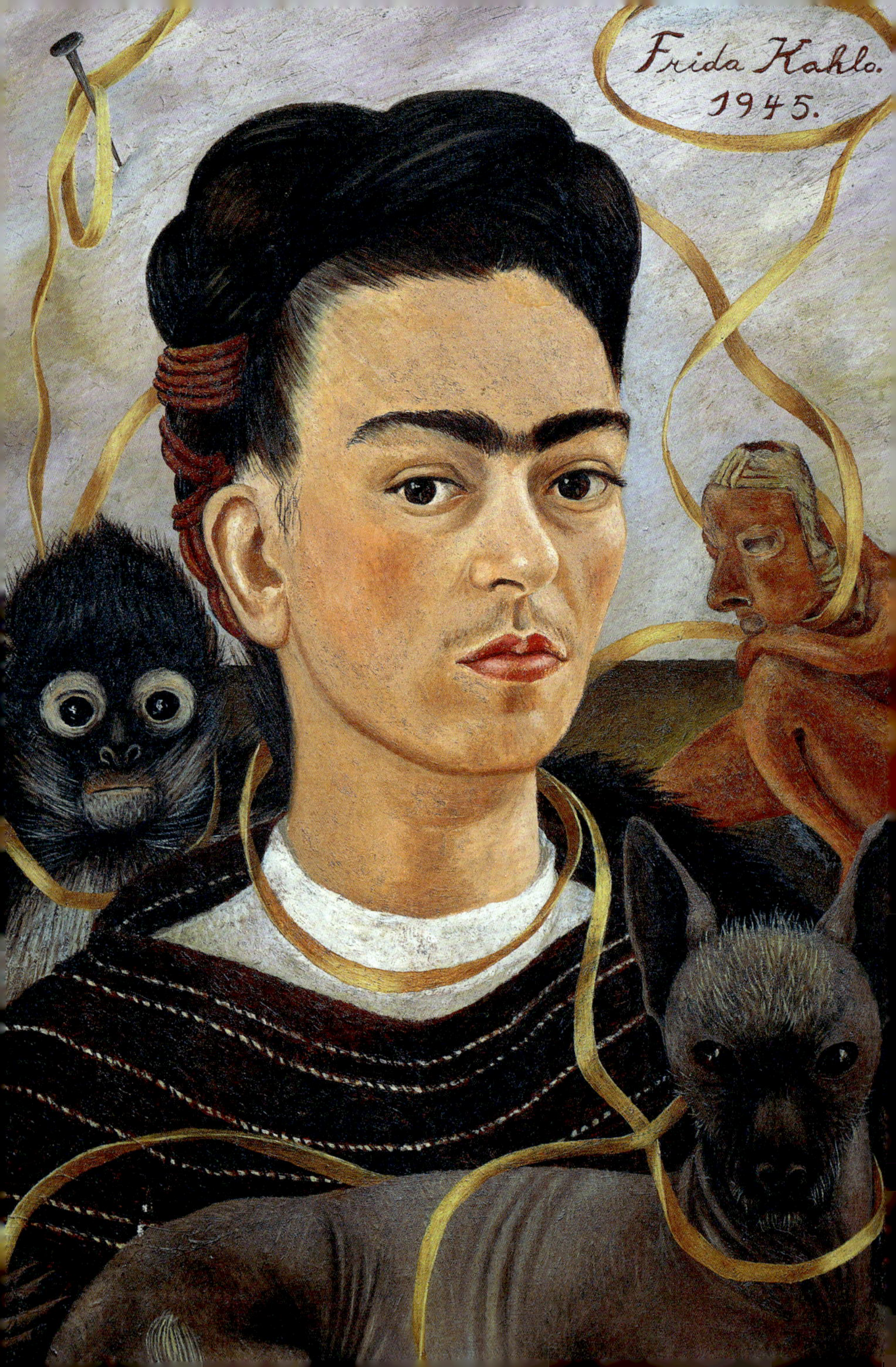
Frida Kahlo.
1945.

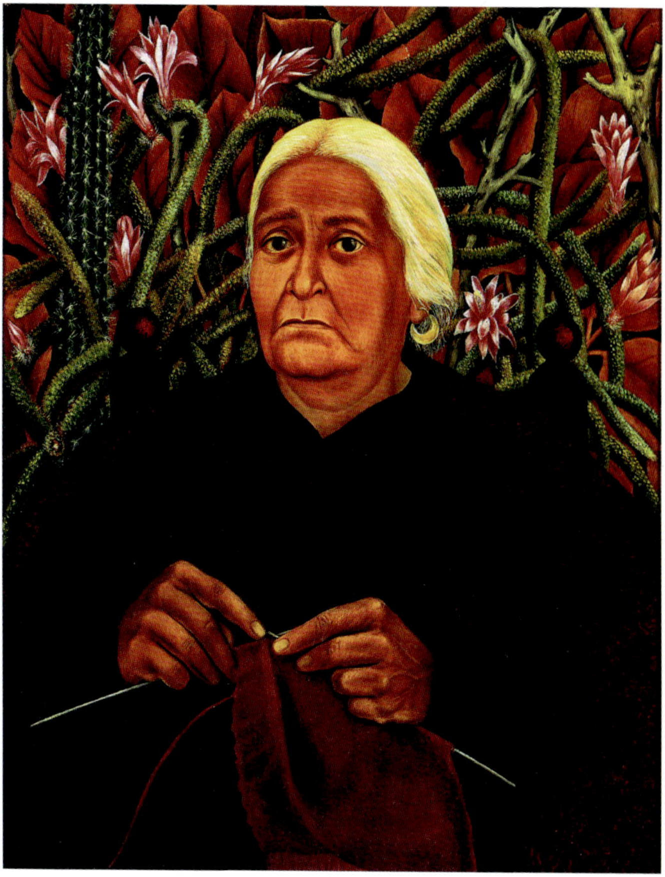

Self-Portrait with Small Monkey 1945
Oil paint on masonite
56 × 41.5

Portrait of Doña Rosita Morillo 1944
Oil paint on masonite
59.5 × 75.5

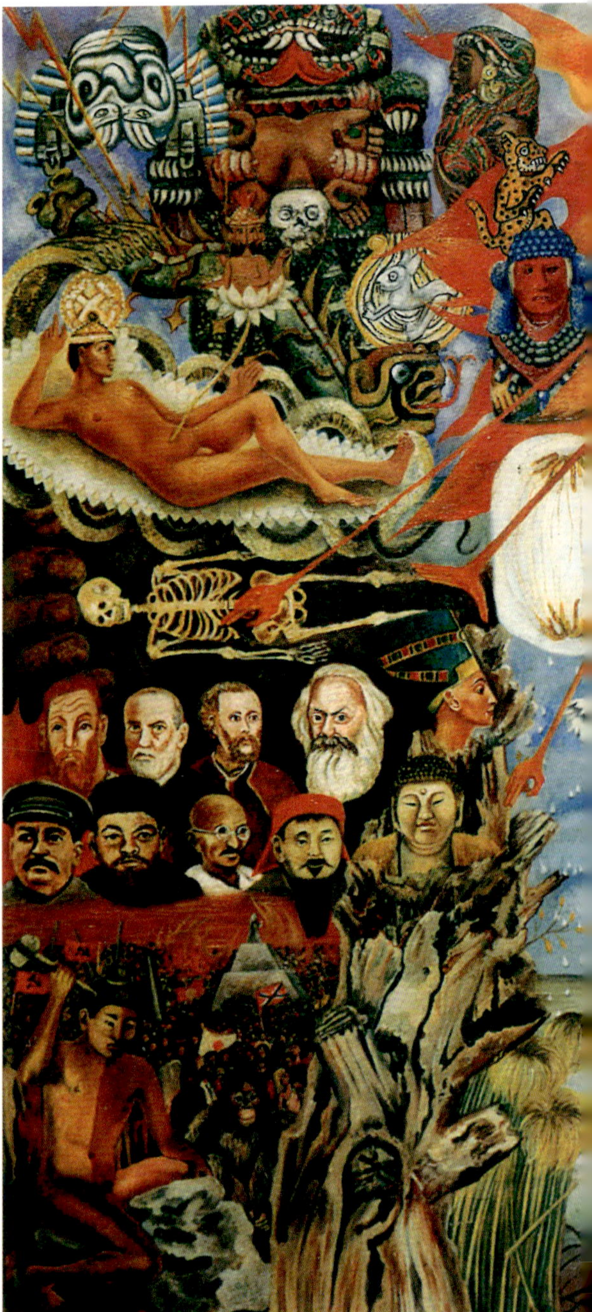

Moses 1945
Oil paint on masonite
61 × 75.6

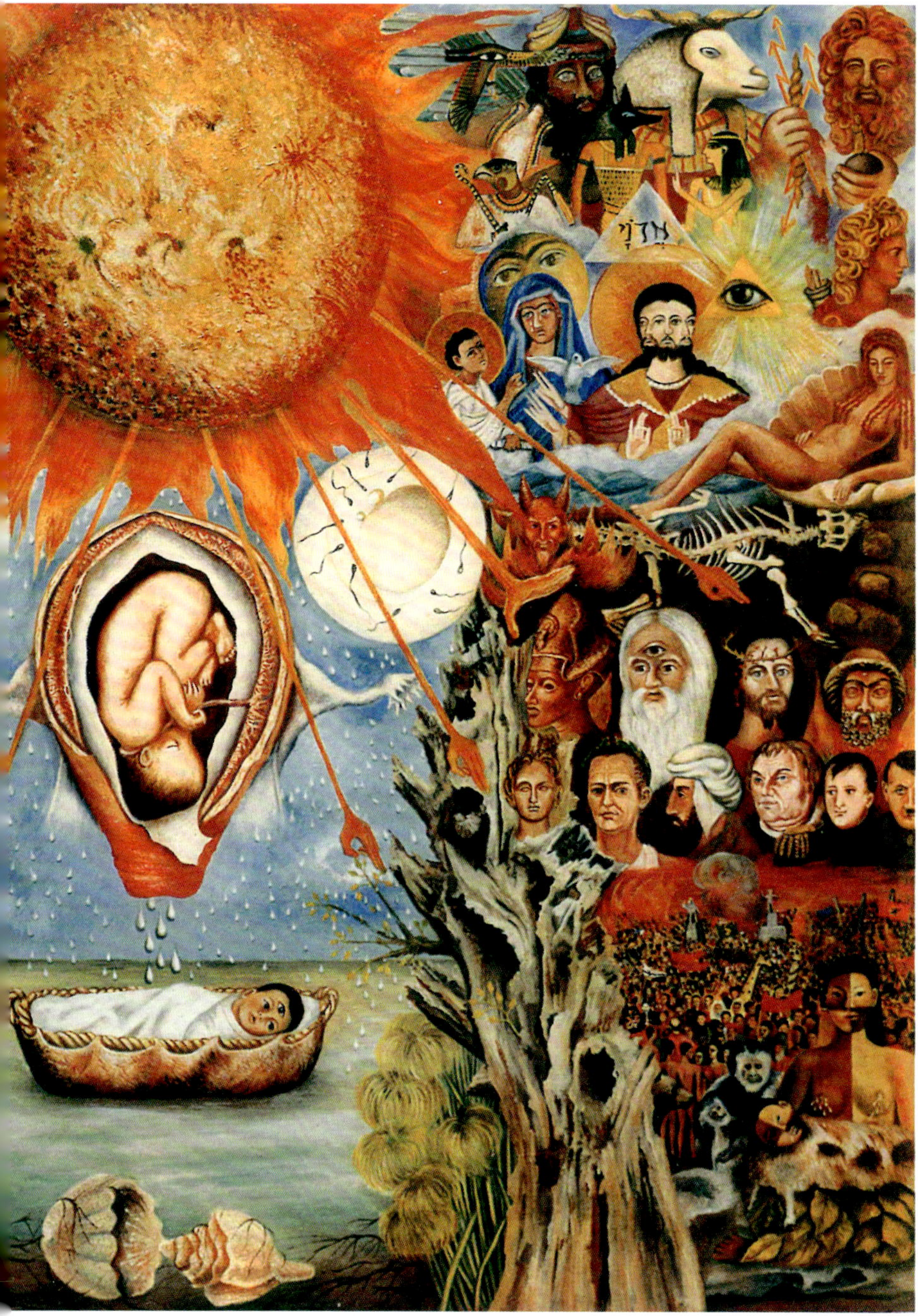

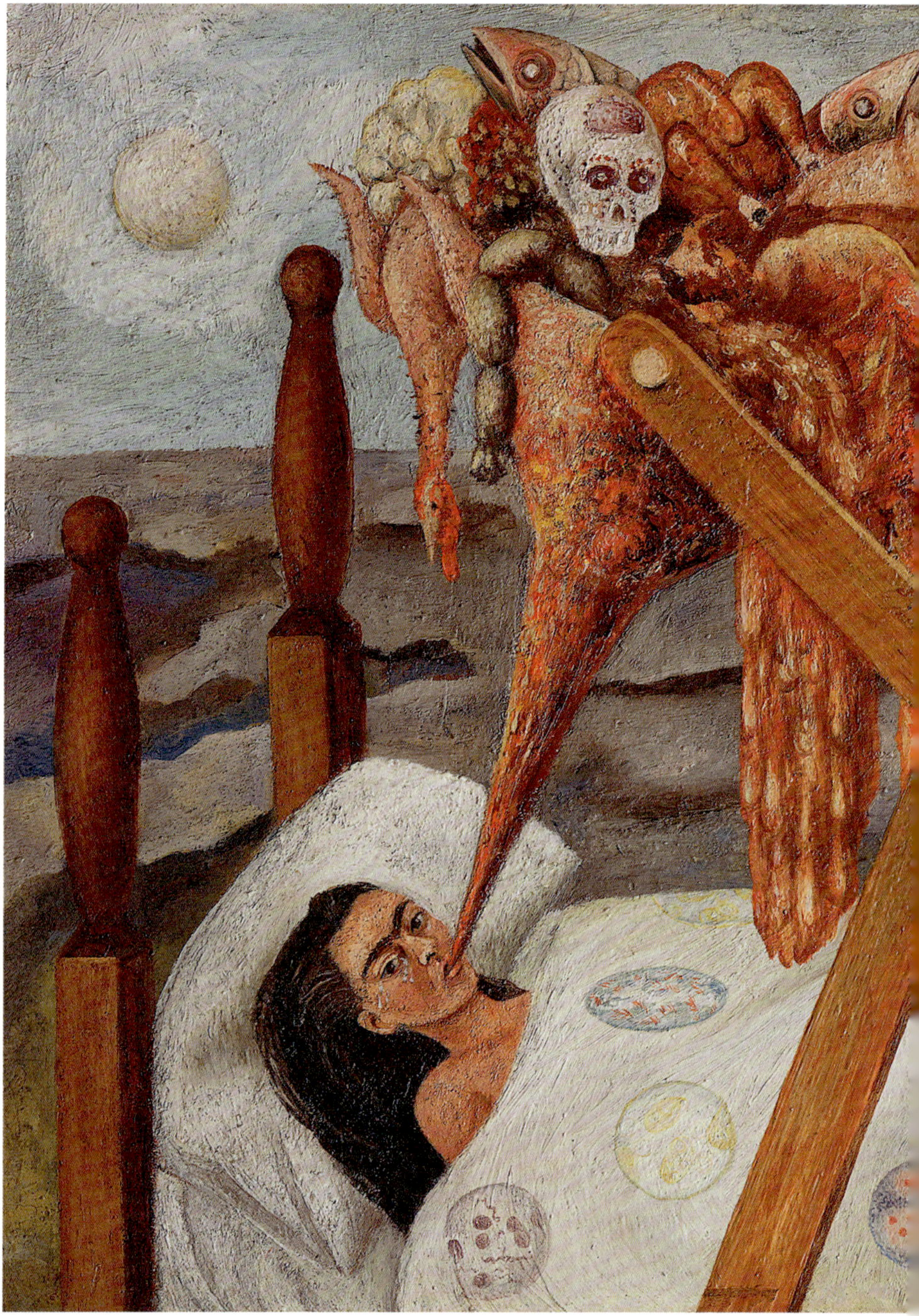

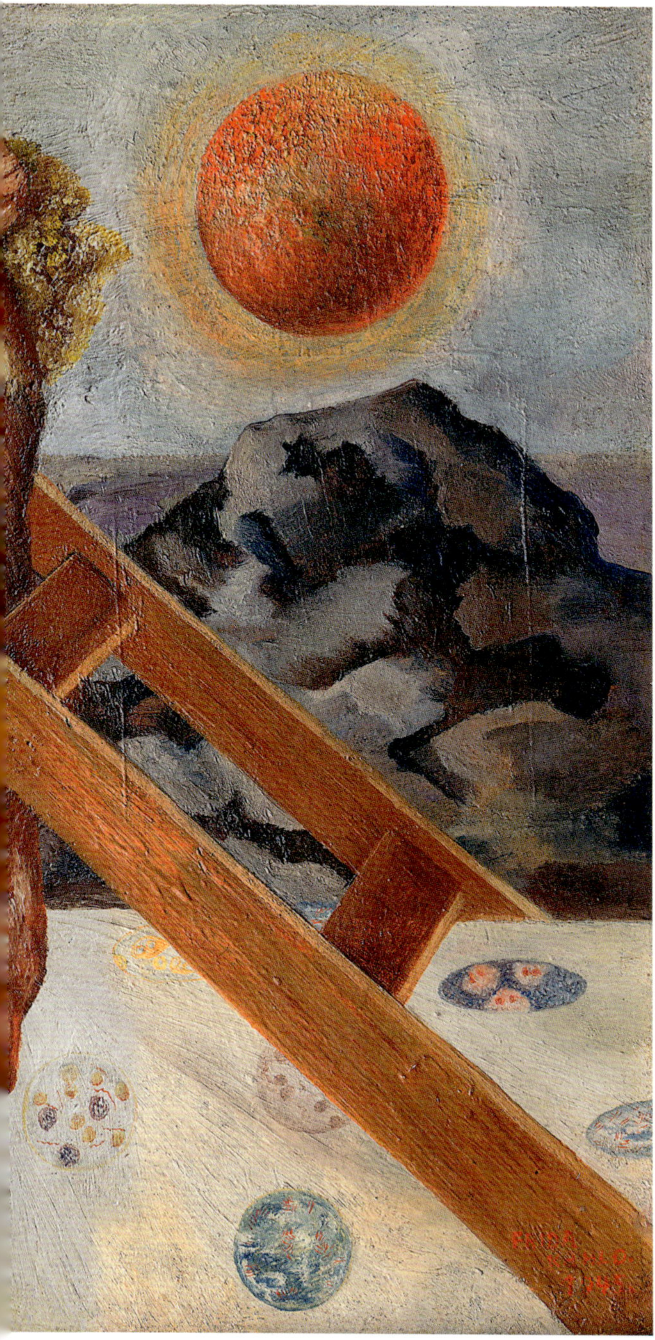

Without Hope 1945
Oil paint on canvas
28 × 36

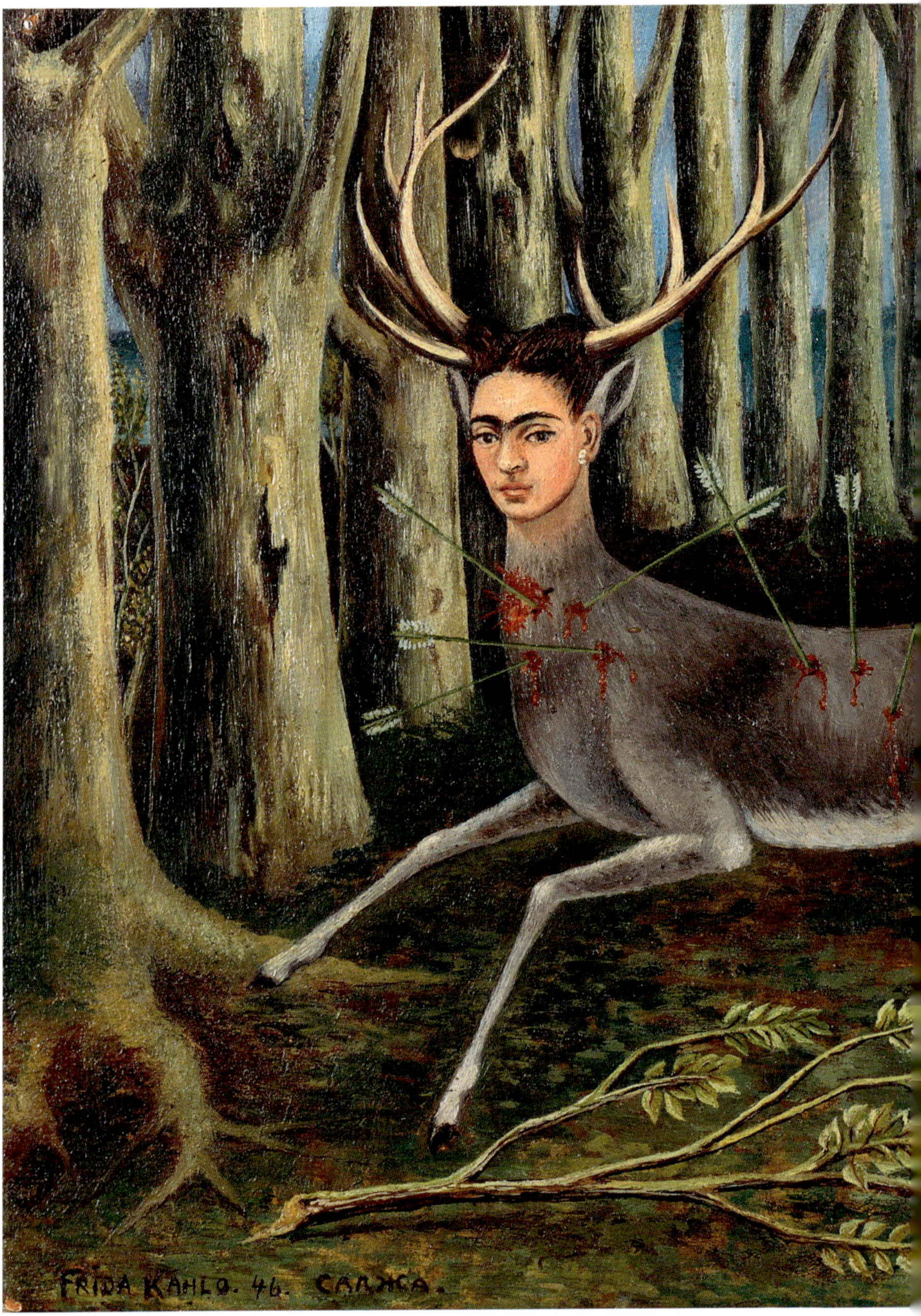
FRIDA KAHLO. 46. CARAJO.

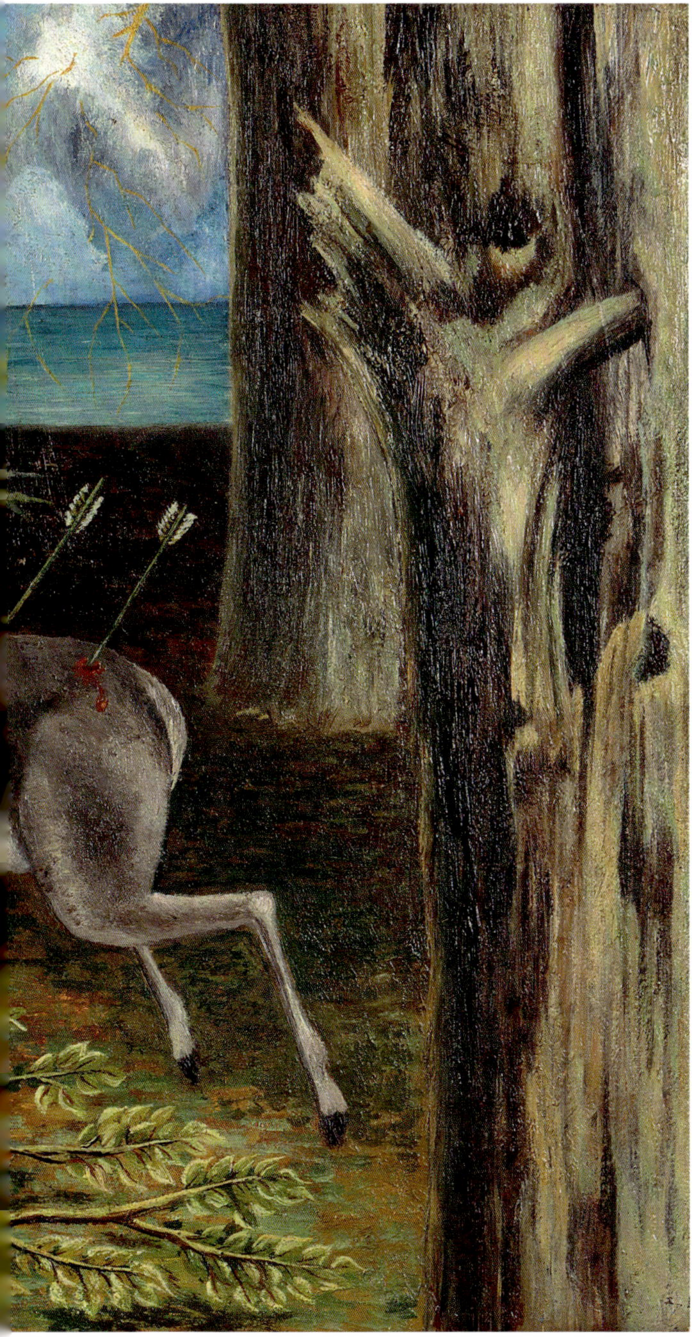

The Wounded Deer 1946
Oil paint on masonite
30 × 22

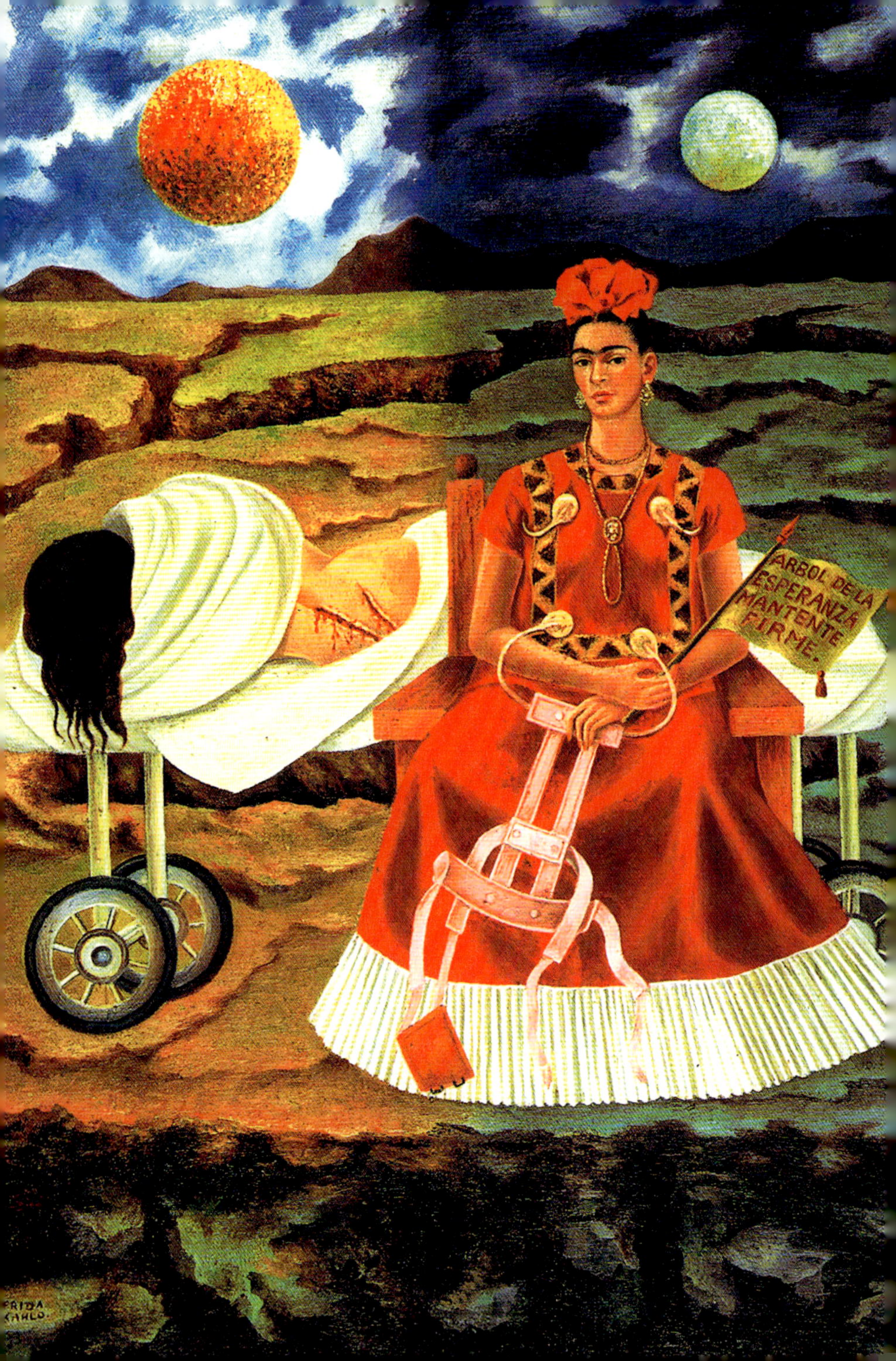
ARBOL DE LA
ESPERANZA
MANTENTE
FIRME.
FRIDA
KAHLO.

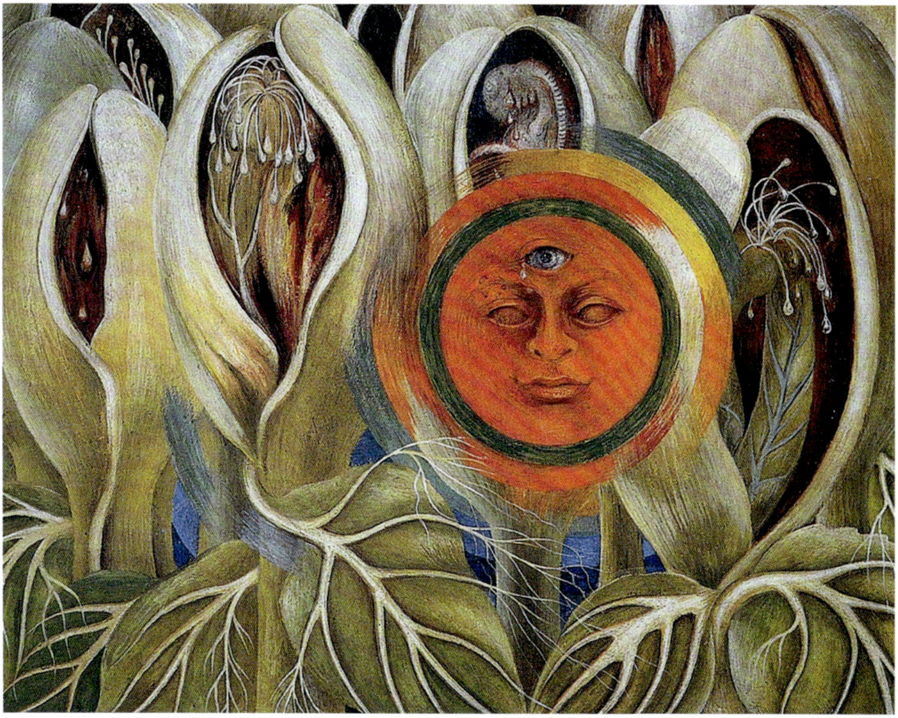

Tree of Hope 1946
Oil paint on masonite
55.9 × 40.6

Sun and Life 1947
Oil paint on masonite
40 × 50

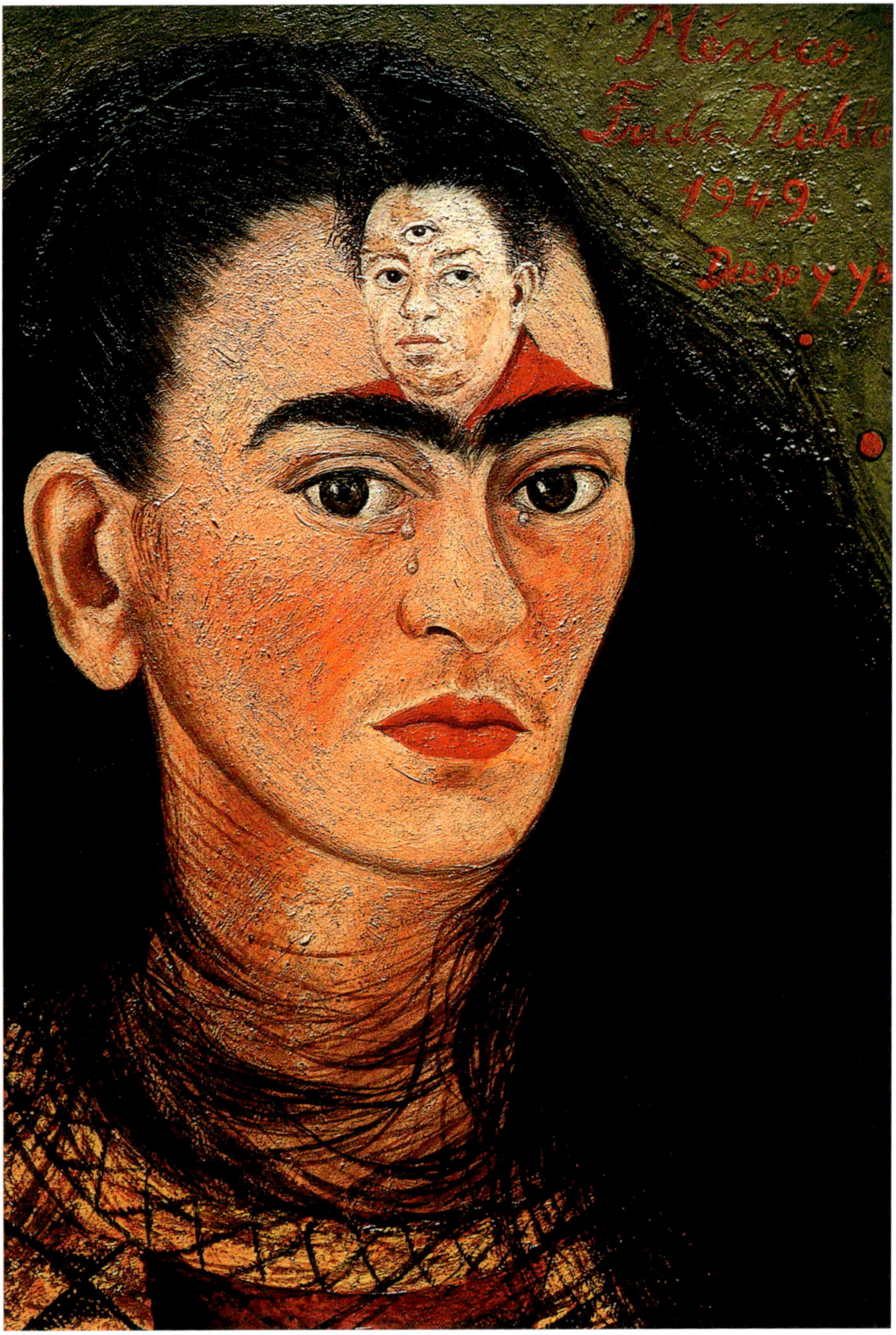
México
Frida Kahlo
1949.
Diego y yo

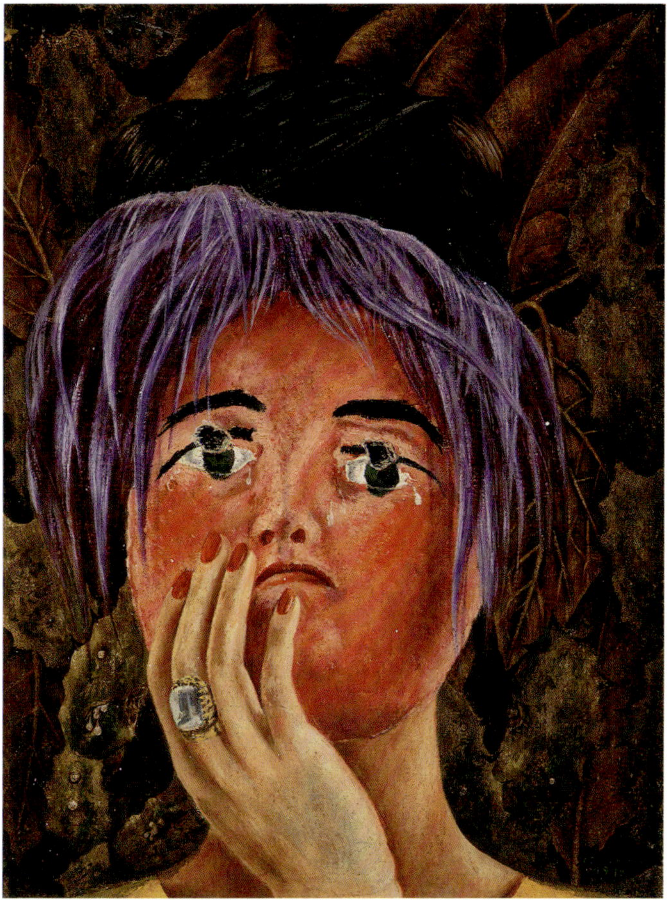

Diego and I 1949
Oil paint on canvas
30 × 22.4

The Mask 1945
Oil paint on masonite
40 × 31

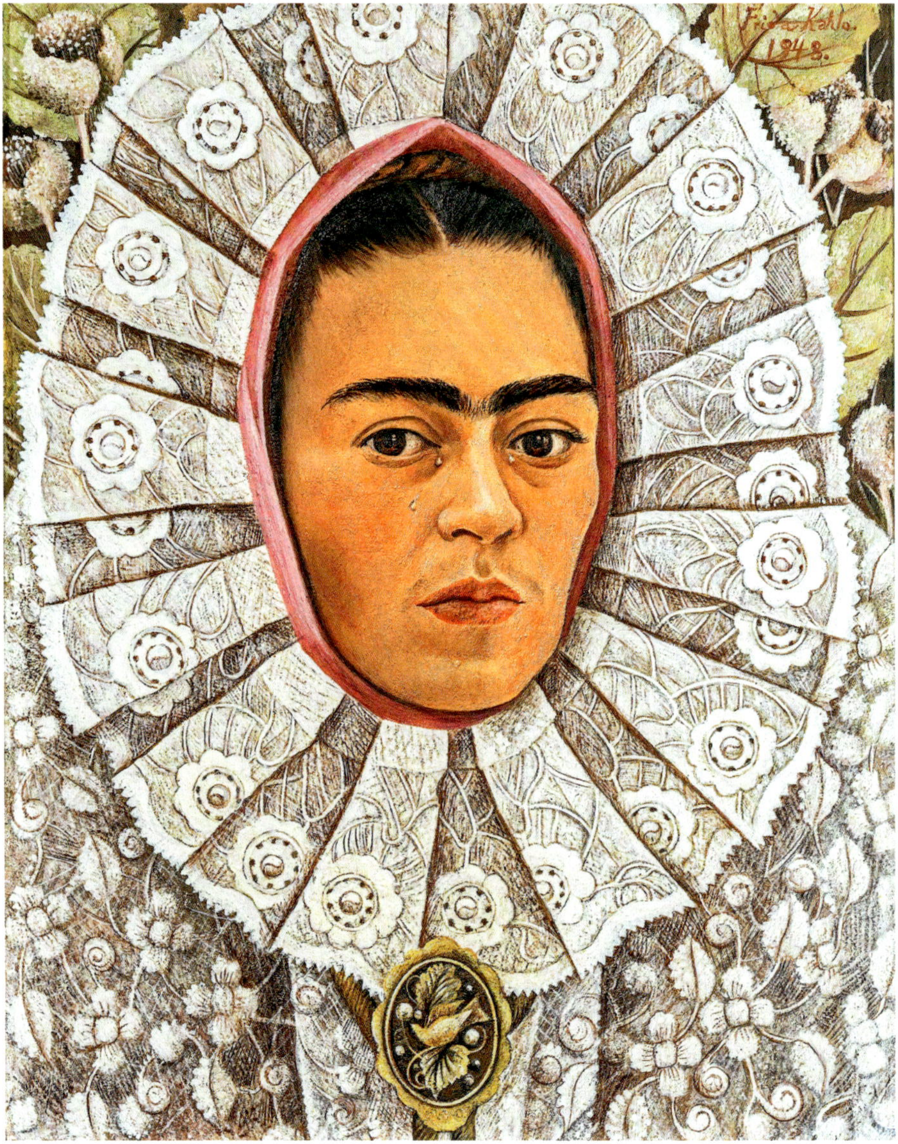

Self-Portrait 1948
Oil paint on masonite
50 × 40

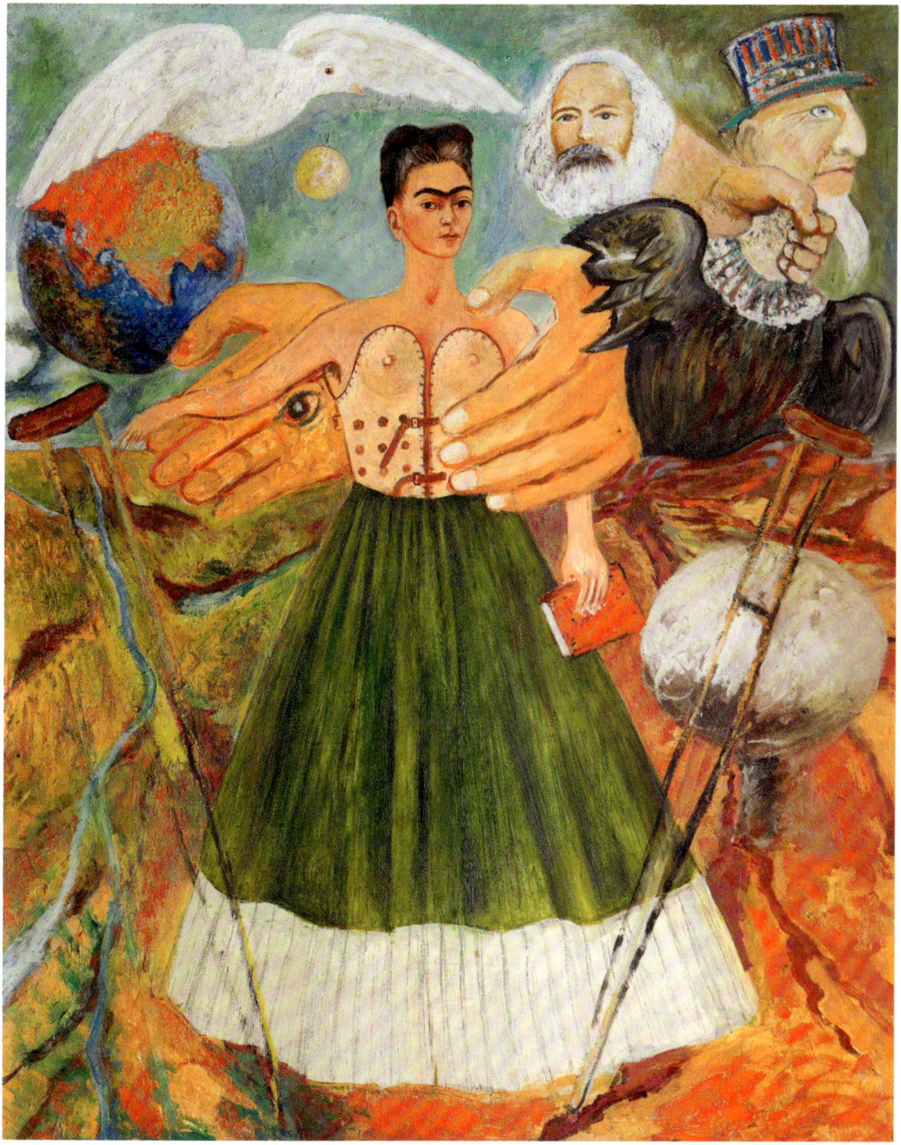

Marxism Will Give Health to the Sick (original title *Peace on Earth so the Marxist Science may Save the Sick and Those Oppressed by Criminal Yankee Capitalism*) 1954
Oil paint on masonite
76 × 61

Self-Portrait with the Portrait of Doctor Farill 1951
Oil paint on masonite
41.5 × 50

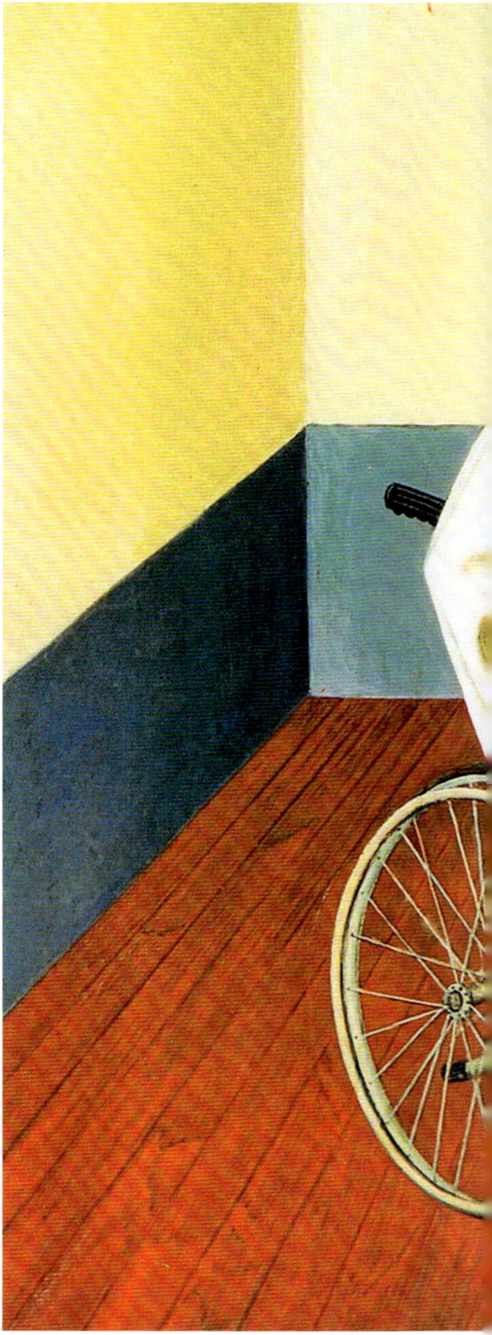

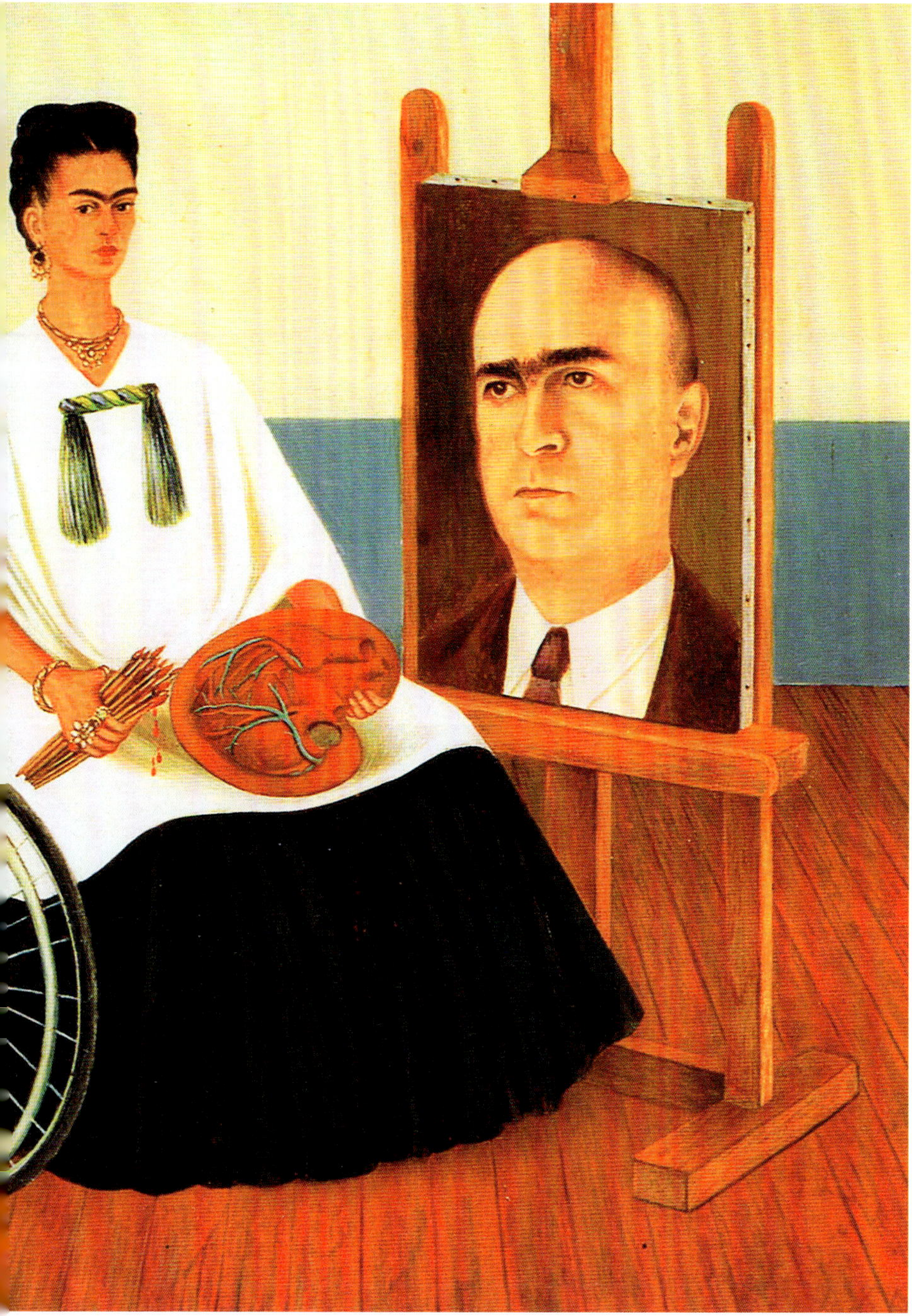

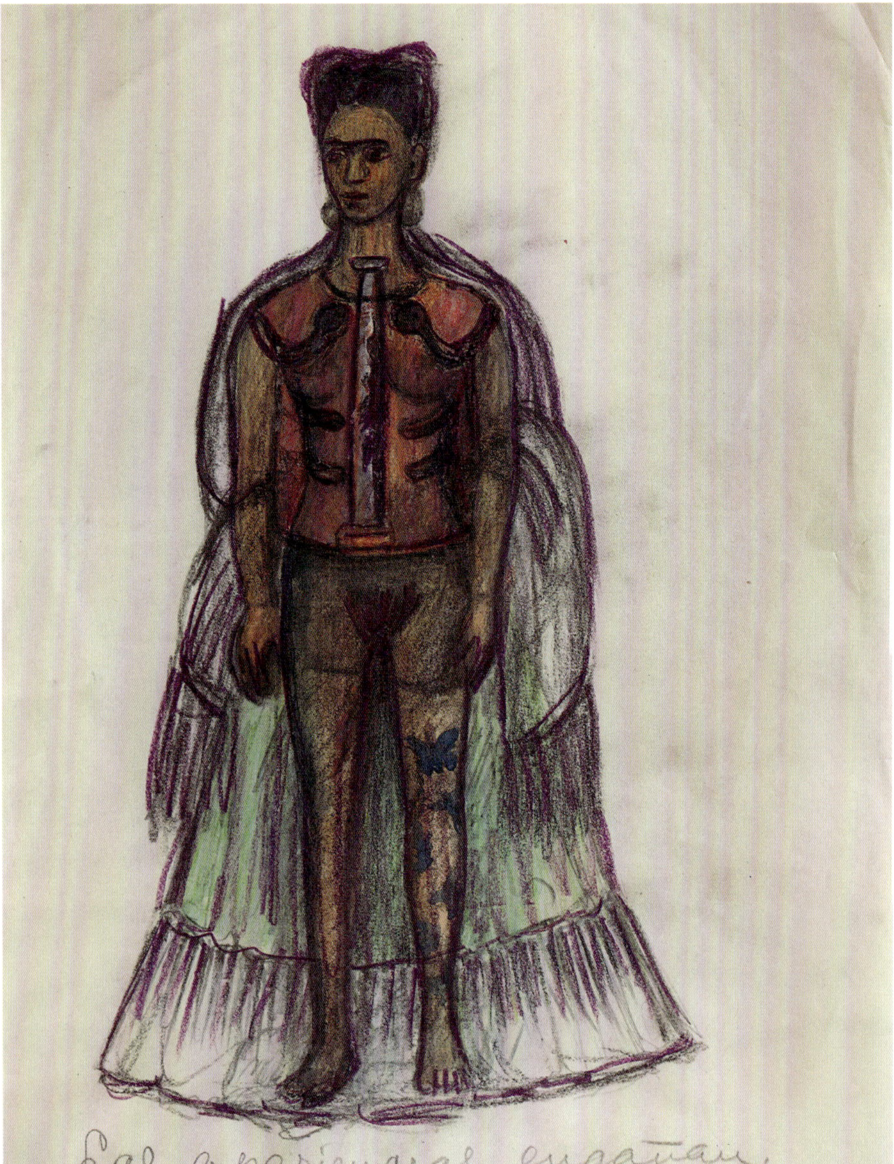

Appearances can be deceiving
1953
Facsimile reproduction
21.7 × 29.8

Feet, what do I want them for, if I have wings to fly 1953
Watercolour in Frida Kahlo's diary
24.5 × 16

OVERLEAF
Viva la Vida, Watermelons
1954
Oil paint on masonite
59.5 × 50.8

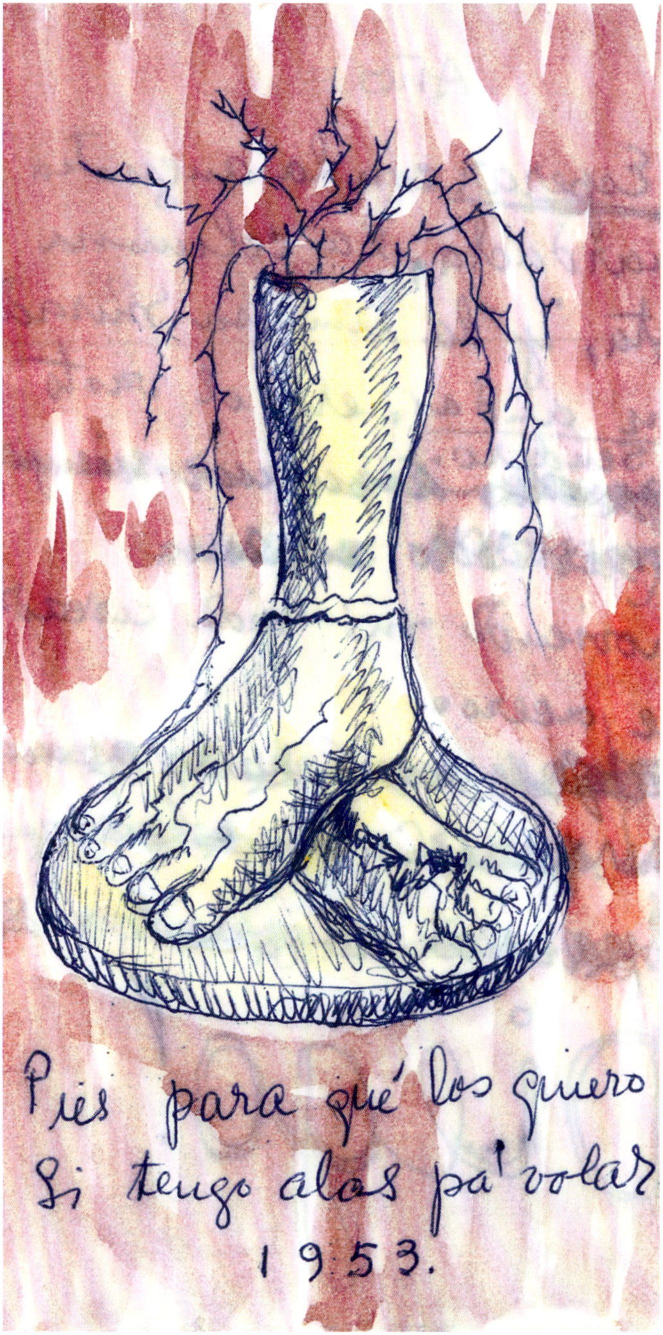

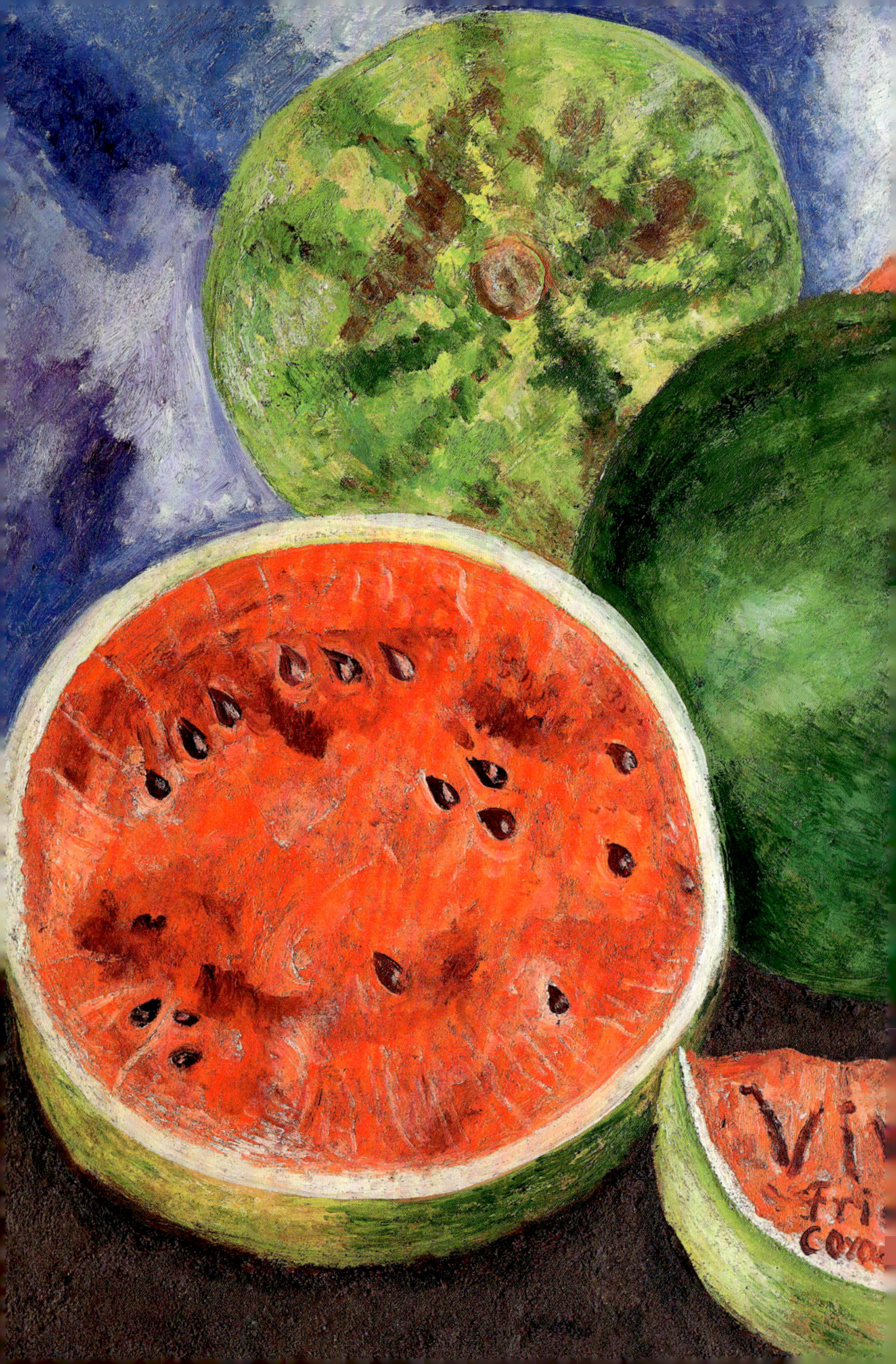

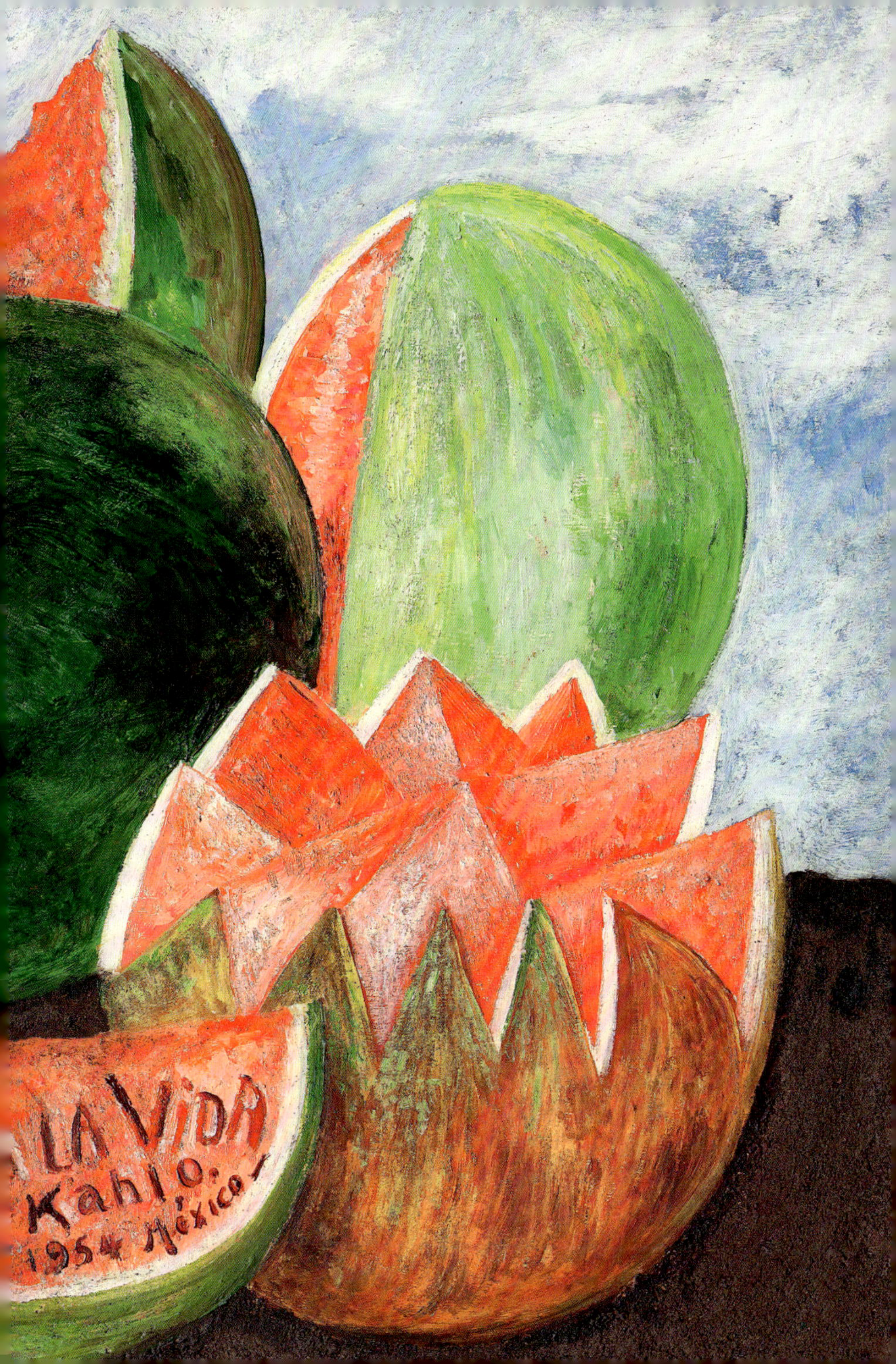
LA VIDA
Kahlo.
1954 México

NOTES

1. Raquel Tibol (ed.), *Frida by Frida*, trans. Gregory Dechant, 2nd expanded edn, Mexico City 2006, p.315. Statement by Frida Kahlo for her application to the Instituto Nacional de Bellas Artes in Mexico in 1945: 'I began to paint out of pure boredom ... I really don't know if my paintings are surrealist or not, but I do know that they are the frankest expression of myself.'

2. Lola Álvarez Bravo, quoted in Hayden Herrera, *Frida Kahlo: The Paintings*, New York 1991, p.10.

3. Nahui Olin, *Óptica Cerebral: Poemas Dinámicos*, Mexico City 1922, p.29. Translation by the author.

4. Hayden Herrera, 'Frida Kahlo's Legacy', in *Frida Kahlo*, ed. Elizabeth Carpenter, exh. cat., Walker Art Center, Minneapolis 2007, p.77.

5. Ibid.

6. Kahlo refers to herself as 'the great concealer' in a diary entry dated 8 December 1938. *El Diario de Frida Kahlo*, ed. Carlos Fuentes, La Vaca Independiente, Mexico, 1994, p.270. The 'appearances can be deceiving' text accompanies a self-portrait drawing found at La Casa Azul.

7. The text is inscribed in Frida Kahlo's *Self-Portrait with Loose Hair* 1947.

8. 'Cuates' is a colloquial Mexican term for 'friends'. The paintings of Adriana Kahlo, Ruth Quintanilla and Jesús Ríos y Valle were destroyed.

9. Other members of the group were José Gómez Robleda, Manuel González Ramírez, Agustín Lira, Alfonso Villa, and the only other girl, Carmen Jaime.

10. Extract from 'Memory', a poem published in *El Universal Ilustrado. Suplementos culturales*, 30 November 1922; reproduced and translated in Raquel Tibol, 'Pain – Love – Liberation: Frida Kahlo's Words', in *Frida Kahlo*, ed. Emma Dexter and Tanya Barson, exh. cat., Tate, London 2005, p.183. Modifications to the translation by the author.

11. See, for instance, letter to Isabel Campos, New York, 6 November 1933, in Tibol (ed.) 2006, p.137, or letters to Doctor Leo Eloesser in ibid., pp.104–6. 'Gringo' is a term for an American, non-Hispanic, white person, sometimes used pejoratively.

12. Florence Davies, 'Wife of the Master Mural Painter Gleefully Dabbles in Works of Art', *The Detroit News*, 9 February 1933.

13. Gannit Ankori positions this work as an 'anti-Nativity scene'. See Ankori, *Imaging Her Selves: Frida Kahlo's Poetics of Identity and Fragmentation*, Westport, CT 2002, p.158.

14. Scholars have also noted the parallels of the scene with the Tlazolteotl Aztec birthing figure.

15. Kahlo changed her name from the Germanic 'Frieda' to 'Frida' during her trip to Paris in 1939.

16. For a discussion on gender identity and Kahlo's identification with the archetypal figures of La Llorona and La Malinche, see Ankori 2002.

17. Kahlo had worn men's clothes early on, as shown in a family photograph from c.1926; reproduced in 'Photographs', in Tibol (ed.) 2006, p.5. In her *Portrait of Irene Bohus* 1947, Kahlo renders her friend with male genitalia and phalluses for arms.

18. Letter to Diego Rivera, 11 June 1940; reproduced in Tibol 2005, p.193.

19. Julien Levy, quoted in Hayden Herrera, *Frida: A Biography of Frida Kahlo*, London 2003, pp.259–60.

20. Ibid., p.135.

21. *El Diario de Frida Kahlo* 1994, p. 235.

22. Herrera 2003, p.266.

23. Kahlo quoted in Herrera 2003, p.252.

24. Herrera 1991, p.180.

25. In Spanish, 'still life' literally translates as 'dead nature' ('naturaleza muerta'). Kahlo inverted the adjective to underscore the liveness of non-human beings ('naturaleza viva'). The term is inscribed on the painting *Living Nature* 1952. Kahlo read Walt Whitman's poetry avidly, sharing his vision of the interconnectedness of all living beings. A copy of *Leaves of Grass* (1886) can still be seen in the bookshelf of her studio at La Casa Azul.

26. Kahlo had a copy of P. Thomas's book, *Hindu Religion, Customs and Manners* (Bombay 1956), in her library. Rivera portrayed her holding a yin-yang symbol in his mural *Dream of a Sunday Afternoon in Alameda Central Park* 1946. Kahlo mentions interest in Taoism in a letter to Dr Leo Eloesser, 11 February 1950.

27. Frida Kahlo, 'Portrait of Diego' [1949], in Tibol (ed.) 2006, p.345.

28. *El Diario de Frida Kahlo* 1994, p.274.

29. Kahlo [1949], pp.347–8. Although this was written by Kahlo in her text 'Portrait of Diego' [1949], this description can just as well be applied to her relationship to nature and the cosmos.

30. Letter to Carlos Pellicer, November 1947, in Tibol (ed.) 2006, p.331.

31. Carlos Pellicer, 'Tres sonetos a Frida Kahlo' in Pellicer, *Obras: Poesía*, ed. Luis Mario Schneider, Fondo de Cultura Económica, Mexico 1981, p.633. Translation by the author. The author first encountered the sonnet in a line referenced by Carlos Monsiváis in his text 'Introduction: Frida in the Land of Self-Portraits' in *Frida Kahlo*, ed. Luis-Martín Lozano, Bullfinch Press, Boston, New York, London, 2001. Monsiváis's text has been influential for this publication.

32. Letter to Alejandro Gómez Arias, 25 December 1924, in ibid., p.34.

INDEX

Page references in *italics* indicate images.

CREDITS

Colección Pérez Simón,
México 44

Collection of Juan Rafael
Coronel Rivera, Mexico
City, Mexico 26

De Young Museum,
Museum purchase,
Dr. R. Earl Robinson Estate
and Achenbach Foundation
for Graphic Arts
Endowment Fund 1996.38
31

Private Collection 10, 46–7

First published 2025 by order of the Tate Trustees
by Tate Publishing, a division of Tate Enterprises
Ltd Millbank, London SW1P 4RG
www.tate.org.uk

A catalogue record for this book is available from the British Library

ISBN 978 1 84976 996 9

Distributed in the United States and Canada by ABRAMS, New York

Library of Congress Control Number applied for

Commissioning Editor: Emma Poulter
Project Editor: Aki Gurung
Production: Juliette Dupire
Picture Research: Sarah Tucker
Designed by Astrid Stavro Studio
Colour reproduction by DL Imaging, London
Printed and bound in Italy by Printer Trento, S.r.l.

Cover: *The Frame* 1938 (detail, see p.51)
Frontispiece: Lola Álvarez Bravo, *Frida looking into a mirror* c.1944

Measurements of artworks are given in centimetres, height before width and depth

MIX
Paper | Supporting responsible forestry
FSC® C015829
FSC www.fsc.org

THE AUTHOR

Beatriz García-Velasco Bernal is Assistant Curator, International Art at Tate Modern. She has worked on a range of exhibitions, live performances, commissions and film programmes, and develops the Tate collection through the Latin American Acquisition Committee. Selected projects include *Frida Kahlo: The Making of An Icon* (2026); *Mike Kelley: Ghost & Spirit* (2024–5); *Capturing the Moment* (2023–4); and *Cecilia Vicuña: Brain Forest Quipu* Hyundai Commission (2022–3). Through her involvement with Tate Film, Beatriz has also worked with pioneering living artists. She is editor and writer of publications including the *Capturing the Moment* exhibition catalogue and the *Preemptive Listening* special issue of the *Disclaimer* journal.

PHOTO CREDITS

2025 © Album / Scala, Florence. Museo Frida Kahlo, Mexico City 86

Album / Alamy Stock Photo cover, 16, 34–5, 36, 45, 51, 53, 59, 61, 62, 64, 65, 66, 88–9

Album / Scala, Florence 24, 50, 72–3, 80

Archivart / Alamy Stock Photo 12, 27, 39, 52, 60, 78, 84–5

Artepics / Alamy Stock Photo 15

Christie's Images, London / Scala, Florence 28–9

Digital image, The Museum of Modern Art, New York / Scala, Florence 42–3

Dom Slike / Alamy Stock Photo 2

© Detroit Institute of Arts / Bridgeman Images 10

Francisco Armando Kochen Beristain 26

Frank Nowikowski / Alamy Stock Photo 63

Heritage Image Partnership Ltd / Alamy Stock Photo 40–1

IanDagnall Computing / Alamy Stock Photo 4, 38, 83

Image courtesy of Sotheby's 68–9

Impaint / Alamy Stock Photo 54–5, 58, 82

Jorge Contreras Chacel / Bridgeman Images 32–3

© NPL - DeA Picture Library / Bridgeman Images 70

Photo © Fine Art Images / Bridgeman Images 76–7

Photo Scala Florence / Heritage Images 74–5

Photo Schalkwijk / Art Resource / Scala, Florence 30, 37, 67, 71, 81, 87

Photograph by Randy Dodson, courtesy of the Fine Arts Museums of San Francisco 31

Private Collection 87

Private Collection Christie's Images / Bridgeman Images 48–9

Rafael Doniz 44

ROBERT / Alamy Stock Vector 21

The Artchives / Alamy Stock Photo 7, 9, 13, 19, 56–7, 79